Twayne's English Authors Series

Sylvia E. Bowman, *Editor*

INDIANA UNIVERSITY

Nicholas Rowe

TEAS 200

Nicholas Rowe

NICHOLAS ROWE

By ANNIBEL JENKINS

Georgia Institute of Technology

TWAYNE PUBLISHERS

A DIVISION OF G. K. HALL & CO., BOSTON

Library of Congress Cataloging in Publication Data

Jenkins, Annibel.
  Nicholas Rowe.

  (Twayne's English authors series; TEAS 200)
  Bibliography: p. 159–63.
  Includes index.
  1. Rowe, Nicholas, 1674–1718—Criticism and interpre-
tation.
PR3671.R5J4   822'.5   76-53826
ISBN 0-8057-6663-4

For my nephew Rob

"His mother, between laughing and chiding, would have put him out of the room; but I would not part with him so. I found upon conversation with him, though he was a little noisy in his mirth, that the child had excellent parts, and was a great master of all the learning on the other side eight years old."

— *The Tattler*. No. 95
Thursday, November 17, 1709.

Contents

About the Author

Annibel Jenkins received the undergraduate degree from Blue Mountain College (Blue Mountain, Mississippi) and an M.A. degree from Baylor University (Waco, Texas). She holds the Ph.D. degree from the University of North Carolina at Chapel Hill.

Ms. Jenkins has taught at Blue Mountain College, Wake Forest College, and Mississippi College. She has taught music, directed plays for school and amateur groups, and participated in and read papers for South Central Modern Language Association, Southeastern Modern Language Association, and the Southeastern Renaissance Conference.

Ms. Jenkins received a grant from the Georgia Tech Foundation for the research and travel necessary for this TEAS study of Nicholas Rowe. She is secretary-treasurer of the Southeastern American Society for Eighteenth Century Studies and is currently working on a critical biography of Mrs. Elizabeth Inchbald, the eighteenth century actress, playwright, and novelist.

Preface

Nicholas Rowe, while seldom the center of discussion, has been mentioned in almost every study of any kind of the eighteenth-century literary or political scene since his untimely death in 1718 at the age of forty-four. The judgments that have been made about Rowe, however, have been for the most part inconclusive and have been drawn largely in the context of his association with other and more celebrated figures like Joseph Addison and Alexander Pope. If the analysis is of Rowe's work, he is chiefly remembered as a transitional writer whose plays were a continuation of the heroic drama of the late seventeenth century and a beginning of the sentimental drama that later developed more fully in the eighteenth century.

For at least the first two decades of the eighteenth century, however, Rowe was a major figure in his own right. A gentleman, poet, and scholar, he was called the "soft complaining Rowe" as a compliment to his sensitive poetry; and he was identified as the creator of the "she-tragedy," that particular kind of drama that brought tears of pity to the eyes of the fair beauties in his audience as they identified themselves with the sorrows of the equally fair beauties he created for the stage. Three of his plays, *Tamerlane, Jane Shore,* and *The Fair Penitent,* have been in print almost continuously since their original publication; and, for well over a century after their presentation, they remained important plays in the repertoires of the major companies in England and America.

This study is, however, the first full-length one of Rowe and of all his work since his fair admirers laid aside their two-volume, leather-bound copies of his *Works* and gave their attention to Lord Byron and the Romantics. Any serious analysis of Rowe and his work must begin by placing him in the context of his time, by showing him as an important member of the literary scene during the Queen Anne period, and by explaining how his work, typical of its own contemporary interests, helped provide the milieu for the development of the more widely known and remembered literature of the Augustan Age. This study proposes, therefore, to make such an introduction.

A first reading of Rowe's plays suggests that they were admired because of their extravagant and melodramatic attention to love, honor, and valor—all qualities of the heroic dramas long popular in the theater of the late seventeenth century. The familiar characteristics were, however, merely frames for the more significant themes of political, religious, and social issues developing among the rising middle-class audience of the post-Restoration theater. The early eighteenth century, the Queen Anne period, provided the basis for the continuation of the Revolution Settlement that established the constitutional monarchy, the broadening view of religion that finally began to give the individual true religious freedom, and the economic opportunities that provided the middle class with the leisure and the means to explore literature and the theater. In all three areas, Rowe was spokesman for his world; but his work reveals far more than his own personal views.

Because his plays, to a much greater extent than his poetry and translations, provide a mirror for his world, this study is chiefly concerned with them. Moreover, the plays have continued to be read by students of English literature, if not by a wide public, and they offer a body of material by which Rowe may be judged. Therefore, while the miscellaneous verse is reviewed and the translations are discussed briefly in this study, the focus of attention is on the plays. Indeed, the plays themselves provide the best examples for judging Rowe as a poet since all six of the major plays, tragedies written in verse, provide ample opportunity for a judgment of Rowe as a poet as well as a dramatist.

The basic premise of this study is, therefore, that Rowe was an important literary figure in the first two decades of the eighteenth century and that his work is to be viewed in the precise context of those two decades. It is hoped that such a view will provide the reader with an introduction to that world—the world of Rowe's contemporaries Alexander Pope, Richard Steele, Joseph Addison, and Jonathan Swift. In a series of plays on stage and in print, Rowe reflected in a memorable fashion at least two of the concerns of all of these writers—their continuing debate about the Whig settlement and about the rising middle class and its interests.

While it is never possible to recreate the context of a past time, it seems to me that to set arbitrary standards of judgment against which to view literary figures is to presume a patently esthetic stance that is by its own presumption false. Rather than make such arbitrary judgments about Rowe, I have tried to explain the circumstances and events that surround the individual plays. These circumstances include Rowe's own life, the political and national life of England from 1700 to Rowe's death in 1718, and the circumstances of state and church that can give the reader a basis for making his own judgments of the relative value of Rowe and his work. Because such an understanding of the past is prerequisite to an understanding of the present, I believe that this treatment will provide the reader with material to make his own estimate of Rowe's contribution to the canon of English literature.

To avoid making the documentation of this study a list of page numbers in a book not generally available, I have used the context of the discussion to place the scenes and acts of Rowe's plays, and I have quoted more material directly from the text of the plays than I might otherwise have done had there been a complete twentieth-century edition of *The Works*.

In both contexts—as an understanding of the milieu of Neoclassical literature in the first half of the eighteenth century and as a reflection of popular middle-class taste—Rowe's work becomes important. The following study cannot hope to explore in depth either Rowe and his work or the world in which he lived; it can indeed do no more than offer the reader a brief account of facts and ideas that need far more explanation and consideration than can here be included; but it does so with the hope that this introductory study will encourage additional reading and investigation of Rowe and his work as well as of his place in the world of the first two decades of the eighteenth century.

Many people have helped in many ways to make this book possible, and I am grateful to all of them. My special thanks are due to the Georgia Tech Foundation that provided a generous grant that made possible my research in the British Library; to my colleagues, Professor David B. Comer III and Professor James P. Smith, who encouraged and supported the project from the beginning; and to my sister, Virginia Jenkins Peacock, without whose prodding and advice the study would have remained merely an enthusiasm for Rowe and his *Fair Penitent* and would never have become a reality.

ANNIBEL JENKINS

Georgia Institute of Technology

Chronology

1674   Nicholas Rowe born June 20 at Little Barford, Bedfordshire.

1688   King's scholar at Westminster.

1691   Admitted to the Middle Temple.

1696   Called to the Bar.

1698   Married Antonia Parsons.

1699   Son John born.

1700   *The Ambitious Step-Mother* produced at Lincoln's Inn Fields in December.

1701   *Tamerlane* produced at Lincoln's Inn Fields in December.

1703   *The Fair Penitent* produced at Lincoln's Inn Fields in May.

1704   *The Biter* produced in Lincoln's Inn Fields in November.

1705   *Ulysses* produced in the Haymarket on November 23.

1706   Death of Antonia Parsons Rowe.

1707   *The Royal Convert* produced at the Queen's Theater in the Haymarket, November 25.

1708   Lutrin's translation by John Ozell published with an introduction by Rowe.

1709   Appointed Secretary to the Duke of Queensberry. Edition of Shakespeare published.

1714   *The Tragedy of Jane Shore* produced at Drury Lane February 2. *Poems on Several Occasions* published. Appointed Land Surveyor of Customs.

1715   *The Tragedy of Lady Jane Gray* produced to Drury Lane April 20. Made Poet Laureate on August 1; married second wife, Anne Devenish; appointed Clerk of the Council of the Prince of Wales.

1718   Daughter, Charlotte, born; Rowe died December 6; buried in Westminster Abbey.

1719   Translation of Lucan's *Pharsalia* published.

CHAPTER 1

Early Life and Times

CELEBRATED in the eighteenth century as the translator of Lucan's *Pharsalia* and in the twentieth as the first modern editor of William Shakespeare's works, Nicholas Rowe was considered by his contemporaries to be one of the most important literary figures of his day. But upon his untimely death shortly before his forty-fifth birthday, there appeared only two brief accounts of his "Life": one was by his friend and physician, Dr. James Welwood; the other, by Stephen Hales, was a brief review commissioned by the publisher Edmund Curll for a preface to a hastily prepared memorial volume, *Musarum Lachrymae* (1719).[1]

Dr. Welwood's account is prefixed to the translation of Lucan published by Rowe's widow the year following his death, and it is rather more of an encomium than a biography. In fact, Dr. Welwood himself writes of Rowe, "Never man had it more in his nature than he, to Love and Oblige his Friends living, or celebrate their memory when Dead; what Pity is it then, that for want of Information, there cannot be paid to his name that just Encomium he ev'ry way deser'vd." "What pity is it" indeed that Rowe has become merely one of a list of minor literary figures in the early eighteenth century and that his plays are remembered in brief paragraphs as being tragedies that derive from the greater vigor of the theater of the Restoration period and reflect the theme of the rising tide of sentimentalism in the literary taste of the early part of his century.

When Nicholas Rowe died on December 6, 1718, he was one of the Lord Surveyors of the Customs in the Port of London, Clerk of the Council for the Prince of Wales, Secretary for Presentations to the Lord Chancellor, and Poet Laureate to his Majesty, King Goerge I. Rowe was among the most successful of contemporary playwrights and a friend of such literary figures as Alexander Pope, Richard Steele, Joseph Addison, and Jonathan Swift. Moreover,

Welwood observes in this same Preface that: "Hard has been the Fate of many a Great Genius, that while they have conferr'd Immortality on others, they have wanted themselves some Friend, to Embalm their names to Posterity. This has been the Fate of Lucan, and perhaps may be that of Mr. Rowe."

Dr. Welwood was more nearly correct than he hoped, for the facts of Rowe's life may be briefly recounted, but his personality and his importance as a literary figure are much richer and more complex than has sometimes been realized. He was, for one thing, the representative of a new attitude toward the theater and toward the literary public that was changing rapidly in the first two decades of the century. A writer who combined political, social, and religious themes, he was among those who set the pattern for the first half of the eighteenth century. If he is a minor figure, he is certainly one of more than second-place importance.

An examination of his work placed in the context of his life and in the political and religious interests of his years is a kind of touchstone for an understanding of the theater and of the practice of poetry by those poets who were both writers and public figures. On the whole, this examination in recent years has been done either in terms of showing Rowe's sources for his plays, thus making him seem a rather derivative dramatist, or in terms of showing how he conformed, or rather did not conform, to the Neoclassical judgments of the "rules" of true tragedy. For his contemporaries, however, Rowe represented the "new" theater, the "new" morality, and the "new" and very personal freedom and independence of the rising middle class. His work does derive at times from earlier plays—originality of plot was as yet not demanded of the dramatist—but his "new" morality that defended the beautiful but sinful Jane Shore or Calista of *The Fair Penitent* instructed the playgoers in compasssion and pity while it flattered the virtuous fair who flocked to the playhouse to see his plays. Throughout all his work there is the constant theme of support of the Revolution Settlement that had been agreed upon during the Glorious Revolution but that had to be reaffirmed by ruler and people throughout most of the first half of the eighteenth century.

Although Rowe lacks some of the universal and timeless qualities of Pope or of Swift, he serves to illuminate their milieu. If he did not attain the political power of Addison or the versatility of Steele, his work shows more clearly and steadily, though perhaps more narrowly, the attitudes of their audience than does theirs. In plot, characterizations, and themes, the plays set out the virtues of freedom, of the church, and of England as Rowe and his audience saw these virtues. In addition, Rowe always found a place for the role of the beautiful but tragic heroine. Because of these subjects, it is little wonder that his plays remained popular long after his death.

I   *Early years, 1674–1700*

Nicholas Rowe was born at the home of his maternal grandparents at Little Barford, Bedfordshire in 1674. His mother, Elizabeth, daughter of Jasper Edwards, Lord of the Manor of Little Barford, Bedfordshire, was married to John Rowe on September 25, 1673. Their first child, Nicholas, was baptized on June 30, 1674.[2] The Rowe family was from Devonshire, and the poet's father John was the first of the family to move from there. John Rowe, trained in the Middle Temple, became quite successful in the turbulent closing years of the seventeenth century; for, according to Welwood, he had "very considerable practice at the Bar, and stood fair for the first Vacancy on the Bench, when he died. . . ."

In 1689, the year following the Glorious Revolution, John Rowe published *Benloe and Dalison's Reports,* a compilation of the cases of two eminent barristers of the reigns of Elizabeth and James I. Welwood's comment about this collection is significant in offering an early judgment of Nicholas Rowe's views as well as in recording those of his father, John: the elder Rowe "had the Honesty and Boldness to observe in the Preface, how moderate these two great Lawyers had been in their Opinions concerning the Extent of the Royal Prerogative; and that he durst do this in the late King *James's* Reign, at a time when a *Dispensing Power* was set up, as inherent in the Crown." Such an attitude as this one and the courage to express it were remarkable in 1689.

The last two decades of the seventeenth century were years filled with conflict—first over the Exclusion bills that would have deprived James II of accession to the crown; and, upon the death of his brother Charles II in 1685, further conflict occurred over James's attempt to reestablish his Roman Catholic faith in England.[3] When on February 6, 1685, James II became king, he did so with the enthusiastic support of virtually the whole of England, for only gradually did he reveal his determination to lead his subjects back into the Roman Catholic Church. The first Exclusion bill, designed to deny the throne to James II, had been introduced in 1679; the last one, in 1681. In spite of the fact that, because of the tangled political contests of these Exclusion bills, two prominent leaders were executed and another exiled, the crown had its way, and James II began his reign in complete control. Unfortunately, he badly misjudged the temper of his people, and his brief reign of three years was filled with almost total chaos.

In June, 1685, the Duke of Monmouth, Charles II's illegitimate son, landed at Lyme-Regis in Southwest England; and he was supported in his attempted rebellion against his uncle by many of the lowly Dissenters of the countryside. His attempt failed amidst the execution of many of his humble followers and ended with his own execution on Tower Hill.[4]

The toleration laws offered in the last years of Charles II and the first ones of James II were patently false even though they were endorsed by such famous religious leaders as William Penn and John Bunyan, for tolerance was promoted for the benefit of the Roman Catholic Church, was opposed to the Establishment, and included the Dissenters only by default. When James II, during his first Parliament in 1685, tried to force his views of toleration, his church policies failed to gain public support. Out of these civil and ecclesiastical conflicts arose the two parties, the Whigs and the Tories. In the beginning their alignments were tenuous and shifting. In a broad sense, however, the Whig party was comprised of that new body of middle-class business men, many of whom were, like Daniel Defoe, Dissenters; and the Tory party consisted of the country squires and High Church clergy, who were interested only in maintaining the *status quo*.[5]

By the fall of 1688, the Whigs and Tories alike agreed to oppose James's policy; and, when William of Orange landed at Torbay on November 4 (helped there, the people thought, by the providential Protestant wind that sped him across the Channel from Amsterdam), he was received triumphantly. Deserted by his supporters, James II fled from London on December 11 at three o'clock in the morning, flinging the Great Seal of his office in the Thames River as he left. He did not succeed in his first attempt to cross the Channel to the safety of the French court; but, when he left a second time on December 22, he did not return; and William and Mary, his elder daughter and her husband, the Prince of Orange, were proclaimed the joint rulers of a country now determined to have a hand in its own destiny.[6]

John Rowe was no doubt widely conversant with political affairs; his book and his reputation suggest that he actively approved of the new emphasis on liberty and constitutional monarchy. Moreover, during these years he was determined that his son Nicholas would have a proper education, for he sent him first to a private school in Highgate and then to the famous Westminster School where he was elected in 1688 a King's scholar. In Rowe's time, Dr. Richard Busby was still the headmaster after more than three decades of directing many pupils who had become important men of the government and of the Anglican Church. Known for his strict adherence to the principles of discipline and order, he had guided Westminster[7] through the uncertain years of the Interregnum only to be faced again in 1688 with no less uncertainties as, in the fall and winter months, the swiftly moving drama of political change again occurred.

For Nicholas Rowe and his school friends, surrounded by the political excitement of the changing fortunes of the monarchy, these years must have been memorable indeed. Rowe was later to be known as an ardent Whig; but, as a King's scholar in 1688, he was probably as much concerned with Greek and Latin as with the definition of the new party labels of Whig and Tory. He was only fourteen in the fall of 1688, an average age for the students at Westminster.

The school curriculum was strong in the Classics, and the training of the pupils was conducted in an energetic fashion. The school day lasted some twelve or fifteen hours, most of which were spent in teaching the boys to read and to write Greek and Latin and in encouraging them to become proficient in rhetorical figures, grammatical constructions, and prosody. The masters read and expounded such writers as Homer, Virgil, and Cicero. After the formal hours of class work for the day were over, the students were required to write compositions of their own in prose or in verse in both Latin and Greek. With such unremitting concentration, it is not surprising that the students at Westminster continued their interest in the Classics and literature after their school days were over. It is certain that Rowe pursued all these interests—political, scholarly, and literary—for he combined them in later years in plays and in translations.

Welwood, writing about Rowe's experiences at school, says: "He became in a little time Master of a great Perfection of all the Classical Authors, both *Greek* and *Latin,* and made a tolerable Proficiency in the *Hebrew;* but Poetry was his early Bent, and his darling Study.

He compos'd at that time several Copies of Verses upon different Subjects both in *Greek* and *Latin*, and some in *English*, which was much admir'd, and the more that they cost him little Pains, and seem'd to flow from his Imagination, almost as fast as his Pen" (XIX).

Among Rowe's schoolfellows were Barton Booth, the actor who created several parts for Rowe's plays; William Shippen, the Tory squire, who wrote songs for them; and Erasmus Lewis—all of whom remained Rowe's friends even though he himself did not stay very long at Westminster. Perhaps John Rowe thought the opening months of William and Mary's reign were not the time for training in the Classics but for a more practical education in law. Nicholas Rowe was entered at the Middle Temple in 1690; and, whatever his preferences for poetry and the theater might have been, he continued his legal training until he was called to the bar. But, when John Rowe died in 1692, leaving a legacy of three hundred pounds a year to his son, Nicholas was financially secure enough to follow his own desires. In the years after his father's death, he was concerned with legal and government matters; but he must also have been increasingly involved with the theater. As Welwood explained, ". . . the Muses had stoln away his Heart from his Infancy, and his Passion for them rendered the Study of Law dry and tasteless to his Palate. He struggled for some time against the Natural Bent of his Mind, but in vain; for *Homer* and *Virgil*, *Sophocles* and *Euripides* had infinitely more Charms with him, than the best Authors that had writ of the Law of *England*" (XIX).

Rowe was married in 1698 to Antonia Parsons, whose father, Antony Parsons, was auditor of the revenue. In 1700, he produced his first play, *The Ambitious Step-Mother*, which was acted at Lincoln's Inn Fields by Thomas Betterton's company. William Congreve pronounced it a success, and Rowe was brought forward thereby into the literary world where he remained an important figure for the next two decades.[8]

II *The Literary and Theatrical Worlds of 1700*

In 1700, the literary world of London was a confusing and exciting place; for literature was rapidly expanding its appeal that had formerly been to a small and exclusive audience to a much broader, more inclusive one. The censorship laws had gone through a series of changes by first giving and then restricting freedom of the press until 1695 when the censorship was removed. Thereafter, the

periodical press flourished; and a few years later the single-essay
journal became established and remained a part of the literary world
throughout the first half of the century. The *Term Catalogues* for the
year 1700 still reveal that those interested in religious books and
tracts were in the majority, but Thomas Southerne's *The Fate of
Capua* was advertised in Trinity term along with Oliver Cromwell's
letters that had been translated from the Latin of John Milton.[9]
Since the booksellers were frequently both the printers and publishers, their presentation of an item matched their judgment of the
economics of the trade. Pamphlets and broadsides of verse were
popular items for a public having little money but possessing an avid
interest in theology and in politics.

Four important and influential literary figures of the Queen Anne
period were still virtually unknown in 1700. Richard Steele was in
the army, a captain of the Tower Guard; his first book, *The Christian
Hero*, was not published until 1701. Joseph Addison, one of Rowe's
good friends, was abroad on the Continent in 1700; and Jonathan
Swift, who later was to be a member of Rowe's circle of friends, was
still editing the letters of Sir William Temple, his late patron and
sponsor. It is probable that Swift had already finished writing *A Tale
of a Tub*, but not until after Sir William's death in 1699 did Swift
become a part of the London scene. In 1700, Alexander Pope, only
twelve years old, was living with his parents in Windsor Forest; his
first published work, the *Pastorals*, did not appear until 1709.
Steele, Addison, and Swift were, like Rowe, to be vitally interested
in the world of politics as well as in that of literature; Steele and
Addison were also to be a part of the world of the theater. Steele, in
particular, was to become important as both playwright and man-
ager at Drury Lane, one of the two "official" theaters of London.

The world of the theater was changing as rapidly as that of the
press in the closing years of the seventeenth century. The two
theaters, Drury Lane and Lincoln's Inn Fields, while still regulated
by the government, were very different in 1700 from what they had
been when Charles II had lent them his firm support. For one
thing, the audience that came to the plays had changed; no longer
comprised almost wholly of courtiers and foppish young men about
town, it contained a good number of the rising middle-class profes-
sional men and prominent business men, spectators who demanded
a somewhat different fare from the cuckoldry and profanity of Restoration comedy. This audience understood Rowe and his plays; in

fact, the audience produced Rowe and his plays as well as those of his contemporaries and fellow playwrights, Richard Steele, Colley Cibber, Joseph Addison, and Mrs. Susanna Centlivre.[10]

The change in the world of the theater in 1700 was far more profound, however, than merely the changing audience. By this time, two of the major figures of seventeenth-century drama had finished their work. After the play, *The Way of the World,* was presented in March, 1700, Congreve virtually ceased writing for the theater; and in the spring, on the first of May, John Dryden died. Associated with the beginnings of the heroic drama, he had employed his skill in defending James II so cogently that, upon the accession of the new monarchs, William and Mary, he was deprived of his post as Poet Laureate. Thereafter, he used the skills he had developed at Westminster as a schoolboy and turned to translation in the closing years of his career. He had presented his last play, *Love Triumphant,* a tragicomedy, in 1694. Dryden and Congreve had been two of the most important playwrights of the late seventeenth century; by December, 1700, when Rowe's *Ambitious Step-Mother* was produced, their work as playwrights had ended.

In 1700, moreover, Thomas Southerne produced his *Fate of Capua* in May; his next play, *The Spartan Dame,* did not appear until after Rowe's death in 1719. Thomas Otway and Nathaniel Lee, two popular dramatists of the late seventeenth century, had been dead for several years. The year 1700 was an auspicious one for a new playwright, especially one seriously interested in tragedy. Of Rowe's later important associates in the theater, Colley Cibber was perhaps the most active that year. Cibber's *Richard III* was published in March; he became adviser to Christopher Rich at Drury Lane; and, in December, 1700, his comedy *Love Makes a Man* was presented for the first time shortly before the production of Rowe's play. Both Cibber and Rowe helped make their theater distinctive. In the first decade of the eighteenth century, Cibber was to be identified as one of the important writers associated with Drury Lane; and Rowe became identified with Betterton and his company in Lincoln's Inn Fields.[11]

In the fall of 1700, when the new theater season opened, the audience was probably not vitally interested either in the future development of theatrical practice and dramatic focus or in the influence that Cibber and Rowe would have. The London audience had changed theatrical alignments in the past, however. In 1695, this audience had helped establish Thomas Betterton and his com-

pany at Lincoln's Inn Fields when he had led a group of well-known
players—among them Barton Booth, Mrs. Elizabeth Barry, and
Mrs. Anne Bracegirdle—to form their own company.[12]

Although we may remark upon change at a later date as far as the
theater patrons were concerned, the playhouses were rather as
usual in the fall of 1700. There were still only two theaters of any
real consequence in London; both were staffed by repertory companies; both acted under government patents—that is, they were
licensed by the king and under government control. Rowe was evidently already a friend of Betterton's, already a familiar figure to the
group who followed him to Lincoln's Inn Fields; and, therefore, we
may suppose that Rowe in turn was familiar with all the conventions
of the acting companies and with the dramas they selected to perform.

These conventions and the public taste that supported them had
developed over the years since 1660 when, upon the restoration of
Charles II to the throne of England, the theaters, closed since 1642,
were reopened, and the presentation of plays and entertainments
once again became legal. Two companies were formed, the King's
and the Duke's; they controlled between them a theatrical
monopoly for London. Actresses were introduced upon the English
stage for the first time; and the plays of William Shakespeare,
Charles Beaumont, and John Fletcher were seen again, though
adapted to a new stage and for a new audience.[13] John Dryden and
his brother-in-law, Sir Robert Howard, produced their play, *The
Indian Queen*, in January, 1664; and thereafter Dryden became an
important writer for the theater. Dryden; Roger Boyle, Earl of Or-
rery; Nathaniel Lee; Thomas Otway; and Thomas Southerne wrote
plays and tragedies. Sir George Etherege, William Wycherley, and
William Congreve wrote comedies. Along with the traditional forms
of tragedy and comedy, there was a new kind of entertainment that
combined story, music, pageantry, elaborate scenery, and cos-
tumes—a combination of the epic poetry, the musical recitative,
and the court masque popular earlier in the century. Sir William
Davenant wrote *The Siege of Rhodes* (1656), the first important one
of these "entertainments" that developed into the English opera and
that suggested the characteristics of what came to be called "heroic
drama."

The term "heroic drama" has been used to identify a number of
plays that have been especially identified with the Restoration
period. The contemporary critical authority about these plays was

Dryden, who himself followed the form in some of his early plays and whose critical essays and prefaces contain the most illuminating discussions of the characteristics of the form. The heroic play, like the heroic poem, was concerned with love and honor. Set in far-away, exotic places, the plays were full of intrigues—exaggerated situations were caused by issues and ideas rather than by dramatic incidents. Like opera, the form was largely an artificial one; and it perhaps was, as one critic says, "A cultural phenomenon rather than a literary achievement."[14]

Many of the heroic dramas were written in rhyme, and their characters were types easily recognized. The protagonist was perfectly "heroic"; the antagonist, perfectly evil; the women, either beautiful and perfectly virtuous or beautiful and completely devious. The characters were so flat that they were seldom developed in any way; but the action of the play developed in complicated interwoven incidents that used violence of the most intense and bloody kind. Murder, rape, and suicide were frequent devices used to support the suspense of the action. Since the stage sets for these plays were quite elaborate, painted flats were used as backgrounds. Within these settings there were pageants of various kinds—processions, court scenes, battle scenes, triumphs of kings and emperors who returned with prisoners in chains. Many times the action of the play stopped while trumpets blared and soldiers marched. The hero, god-like in appearance, declaimed his speeches in a formal style of high rhetoric, and this delivery in a kind of musical tone, punctuated with stylized gestures, gave additional support to the whole extravaganza.

One authority of the Restoration drama has observed that

Following the terminology of the age, we will have to call every kind of serious play a tragedy, whether it ends happily or unhappily. But we can distinguish four marked varieties: (1) villain, or intrigue, tragedy, which deals with lust, ambitions, or revenge and places the emphasis upon a villain; (2) heroic tragedy, which is dominated by a character of heroic proportions; and had love-versus-honor as its theme; (3) high tragedy which shows the fall of a great man who is destroyed by his own passions; and (4) pathetic or sentimental, tragedy, which shifts the emphasis from villainy to the sufferings of innocent victims.[15]

Of these four kinds, Rowe was to follow and adapt for his own purpose the "heroic tragedy" and the "pathetic or sentimental tragedy."

To point out these features of the heroic drama does not suggest that it was without merit, but to review such conventions does remind us that Restoration and early eighteenth-century drama was quite unlike our own. In the 1660's and 1670's, when the heroic dramas were written, the audience was very much aware of war; there had been the wars with the Netherlands, Monmouth's rebellion in 1685, and the long war with France from 1689 to 1697. Moreover, the attention to love in the drama was an extension of the popular view of poetry and the long prose romances that were especially favored by the women since the return of Charles II and his court from France. The people's interest in kingship, nurtured by the civil disorders of mid-century, was a constant topic for discussion. The heroic drama, with its combination of all three of these topics, particularly appealed to their taste.

From the time of the sixteenth century and Henry VIII, English citizens, high and low, were especially concerned with religion and with politics. And because the monarchy was continually bound up in the quarrel between the Protestant Church of England and the Catholic Church of Rome, championed by France and Louis XIV (by 1700 considered to be England's chief enemy), the opposition of church and state quite frequently became the center of controversy among the British people themselves. This controversy had become even more intense in the latter part of the seventeenth century when, upon the death of Charles II (1695), James II became king. James II was a Roman Catholic; and, since the king was head of both church and state according to the settlement of the restoration of the Stuarts to the throne, the problem of the king's religion became a major one—to be reckoned with on all levels of discussion.

Moreover, both the stage and the printed play were regarded in a way quite different from our view of the drama. In the last years of the seventeenth century, the periodical press had not developed as it was to do in the first two decades of the eighteenth century. The accounts of battles, political events, natural phenomena such as storms, earthquakes, and the like were printed as pamphlets or broadsides. Fiction was largely found in travel literature or multivolume translated French romance. Poetry appeared as either love lyrics or as satires. The play, both on stage and in print, occupied a place unique—one quite different from its status in our time and indeed from its place by Henry Fielding's time when the novel had begun to develop. The play was a major form for literary expression and for instruction, as well as for entertainment.

To the audience who made the heroic drama popular, its conventions were exciting, entertaining, thought-provoking, and, perhaps, inspiring. The people knew what heroes should be; they debated about kings and conquests daily; they liked to imagine far places; and they enjoyed contemplating love and valor. Even the satiric commentary about the heroic drama in such a play as George Villiers, the Duke of Buckingham's *Rehearsal* (1695) simply helped to promote its popularity. Within the context of public affairs, political interest, and stage fashions, Rowe began his career. From his first play to his last, however, he adapted these interests and fashions to his own ends. By 1700, when Rowe's *Ambitious Step-Mother* was acted, heroic drama was already somewhat out of style; and the pathetic or sentimental tragedy identified almost wholly with Thomas Otway and Nathaniel Lee was never to be as precisely defined as heroic drama; but within these two—heroic drama and pathetic or sentimental tragedy—Rowe constructed his own version of Augustan tragedy.

III   *Rowe and his Friends*

Rowe knew all the major writers of the age of Queen Anne; he was indeed friend and intimate to them, dining with them, writing to them, and discussing, no doubt, the chief interests they all shared in politics and letters. While it is true that Swift finally came to hold very different political views from Rowe's and that Pope, on the whole, avoided partisan politics, they all helped to establish in one way or another the literary climate of the first two decades of the eighteenth century. In their own time, Rowe was an important member of their group.

Rowe's association with these writers—Steele, Addison, Swift, Pope, Cibber—and with many others furnishes a clear though disappointingly incomplete picture of his warm, convivial personality. A wit, a man about town, an ardent Whig—he was all of these. A welcome tavern companion, a welcome guest, a gentleman—he was also all of these. Writing to Stella during his London years in 1710, Swift describes what was probably a frequent occasion when, after dining with Rowe, he relates that "we went to a blind tavern where Congreve, Sir Richard Temple, Eastcourt, and Charles Main, were over a bowl of bad punch. The Knight sent for six flagons of his own wine for me, and we stayed till twelve."[16]

John Dennis, writing in 1715 to congratulate Rowe on his being made surveyor of customs, reveals, perhaps unwittingly, that Rowe was hardly the man to give his time exclusively to the pursuit of business:

I was very much surpriz'd when I saw it in the Publick News. For knowing it to be only a warrant place, and consequently, a place which a man cannot supply by Proxy, I did not understand how it could be compatible either with your Pleasures or with your other Business. However, if you are pleas'd I am so likewise, and once more I congratulate you.

But, Sir, I had almost forgot myself; Instead of congratulating you, upon one office, I should wish you Joy of two. You are become a Husband since I saw you last, as well as a Land Surveyor. Jesu! What Alteration must not those two Offices have made in the Life of a Gentleman, who lov'd to lie in Bed all Day for his Ease, and to sit up all night for his Pleasure. . . .[17]

A gentleman "who lov'd to lie in Bed all Day for his Ease, and to sit up all night for his Pleasure" must have been a welcomed companion with whom to explore the London scene.

CHAPTER 2

The Ambitious Step-Mother:
A Play of Political Intrigue

*T*HE *Ambitious Step-Mother*, Nicholas Rowe's first play, was
presented by Betterton and his company at Lincoln's Inn Fields
sometime late in 1700. As is true of most first productions, the play
was a combination of the features of the tragedies with which Rowe
and his audience were familiar and of new characteristics that
marked it as the production of an important new dramatist. Many of
its outward features matched the general characteristics of the
heroic models that had been popular since Dryden and D'Avenant's
establishment of the genre in the 1660's and 1670's. The definition of
the heroic drama that Dryden himself suggested—"an imitation, in
little, of an heroic poem; and, consequently, . . . love and valour
ought to be the subject of it"—has not been violated; but the emphasis
has been shifted, at least slightly, toward the role of the women and
love and away from the men and valor.

Although an analysis of *The Ambitious Step-Mother* shows that all
of the characteristics of the heroic play are clearly present, the
combination of them becomes a new and quite special one because
of Rowe's own particular interests and techniques. Moreover, in
Rowe's combination of interests his feeling for the pathos—a special
kind of pity and fear—of Thomas Otway and Nathaniel Lee is evident. Rowe wanted the spectator to "go away with pity . . . not
altogether disagreeable to the person who feels it." In a recent study
of the heroic drama, Rowe's heroic qualities and his innovation in
this play are commented upon: "The first acts of *The Ambitious
Step-Mother* seem to be a relatively successful recreation of the
heroic play . . . but by the end of the play another tone has become
dominant. . . . the tragic programme, precisely in line with the
increasing regard for tenderness and pity, is carried out in the second half of the play in striking fashion."[1]

The *Ambitious Step-Mother* has an exotic Oriental setting: its characters are molded in the bold outlines of the sentiments of valor, glory, and honor; its plot is developed by conflict between two equally noble "heroes"; and the theme of love is of equal, if not greater, importance than the themes of ambition and honor. Moreover, the conflict among the contenders for the throne of Persia reminds the audience that disunity and overweening ambition bring about the horror of civil disorder as well as almost certain disaster to the fair and the innocent.

I *The Action of the Play*

The play opens with the plotting of Magas, the high priest, and Mirza, the prime minister, to assist Queen Artimisa in her plan to secure the crown for her son Artaban rather than to honor the prior claim of her step-son Artaxerxes. Since the old king lies dying, he is already beyond controlling the conspiracy of his ambitious queen and the evil and lustful ministers of his government. On this very day, the feast day of the Sun God, Artaxerxes, the elder son and rightful heir, returns from exile with the old general, Memmon, and his beautiful daughter, Amestris. Artaxerxes, exiled with Memmon because of his loyalty to his faction and his love of the beautiful Amestris, has denied both loyalty and love to Mirza's daughter, Cleone, who had been offered to him by her father. From the opening scene of the play, we have not only the complications of a court-intrigue plot but the conflict of love as well. The triangle formed by Artaxerxes' refusal of Cleone and his love of Amestris is complicated by the queen, who would have Cleone marry her own son, Artaban; but Cleone herself, hopelessly in love with Artaxerxes, wastes away in melancholy far from the court.

When Memmon and Artaxerxes enter their native city like unwelcomed strangers, Memmon remembers his past triumphs; and Artaxerxes declares he will not become a slave to his younger brother. Amestris, appearing with her attendants, interrupts such war-like resolutions as those called for by her father; she complains that she must forsake her solitude to contend with "curst Ambition." Artaxerxes assures her that she will be safe with him, and that, when he mounts the throne, he will do so only to share it with her. Indeed, so overcome with love is he that he declares that for her he could almost be content to live obscurely—"forgotten and unknown of all but my Amestris."

Meantime, the queen, her son Artaban, Mirza, and Magas discuss what they will do about Artaxerxes and Memnon. Artaban himself in his first appearance on the stage declares his resolution to fight for his rights; at the same time, he refuses to engage in a battle of words, leaving such a tactic, as he says, to the queen: "Give me my arms, and let us stake at once/ Our rights of merit and of eldership,/ And prove like men our title," (I, 25). Whereupon she is called to exert her rhetoric when Artaxerxes, Memnon, and their attendants enter to confront her with Artaxerxes' request to have an audience with the old king, his father. The queen refuses his request, and Artaban, in the ensuing quarrel, offers to defend his mother's honor as well as his own. Once resolved, however, to meet in battle, Artaban and Artaxerxes agree to cease their conflict until the death of their father.

The third act includes the spectacle and pageantry of the play as mounting tension builds to a climax of violence in the fourth act. When Act III opens, Cleone is lying on a bank of flowers and is singing a sad pastoral about a swain who hears a fair nymph complain. Cleone examines her heart as she talks to her friend Beliza about her love for Artaxerxes. She had fallen in love at first sight of him when she had thought in her inexperienced innocence "that all/ Like me, beheld and bless'd him for his excellence" (I, 35). Beliza reports that she has heard the prince will wed the fair Amestris this very day without any knowledge of Cleone's fateful love and devotion, and she urges her in vain to "let a second flame expel the first." At this moment, Artaban enters to offer himself—his love and passion—to Cleone; and he, unaware of her feeling for Artaxerxes, speaks in urgent words,

> Why dost thou frown?
> And damp the rising joy within my breast?
> Art thou resolv'd to force thy gentle nature,
> Compassionate to all the world beside,
> And only to me cruel? Shall my vows,
> Thy father's intercession, all be vain?   (I,37)

But Cleone replies:

> Oh Prince! it is too much; nor am I worthy
> The honour of your passion, since 'tis fix'd

By certain and unalterable fate,
That I can never yield you a return: (I, 38).

The scene shifts to the Temple of the Sun as the other lovers, Artaxerxes, Amestris, and their attendants come forward from the sacred ceremony that has united them in marriage. Amestris is still caught between joy and fear as the tone of the evil conspiracy is again introduced by her father, Memnon, who cannot be persuaded, in spite of his pleasure upon this occasion, that fate will continue to bring him joy and success. Memnon is correct; evil is the tone, for already, in the most sacred place of the Temple of the Sun, Mirza and the queen congratulate themselves that they have plotted well and have kept their secret from Artaban while they have arranged to secure Artaxerxes, Amestris, and Memnon as prisoners at the close of the sacred rites on this the greatest feast day of the year.

The ceremonies take place as the Hymn to the Sun is sung; and all the people—the priests, the queen and her attendants, Artaxerxes, Amestris, Memnon, and their attendants—bow toward the altar in solemn worship. Immediately after the ceremony, Artaxerxes, Memnon, and Amestris are taken prisoners; Artaxerxes and Memnon are confined in a dungeon; but Amestris, separated by force from her husband, is taken into Mirza's private apartment. As the confusion of parting the bride and bridegroom is enacted, Mirza, speaking aside, reveals his evil desires to have Amestris for his own pleasure.

The fourth act opens with Artaban's refusing to be a part of the evil rebellion of his mother and Mirza; the queen in turn quickly shows her hand as she tells him, "But know, young King, that I am fate in Persia,/ And life and death depend upon my pleasure." While this scene is taking place, Cleone is preparing to release Artaxerxes as she, dressed in a man's habit, uses her knowledge of the palace to enter the prison secretly. When she comes to the prisoners, Artaxerxes and Memnon cannot believe that deliverance is offered them; they think her act to be a trick leading to their destruction. Cleone, in despair as she realizes that even her heroic act of love is misunderstood and discounted, stabs herself. Artaxerxes, catching her as she falls, discovers her identity and mourns her now lost beauty and goodness. But there is no time to lament; and, taking the key she has given them, they prepare to escape into the open city.

The first scene of Act V presents a brief conversation between Mirza and Magas as the priest and the evil minister, respectively, who must now take into account the mood of the crowd which threatens to forsake the new king, Artaban, and to give its favor to Artaxerxes. Mirza refuses, however, to give his attention to the situation; for he has secretly planned to enjoy the beauteous Amestris who is now a prisoner in his private apartments in the palace. In the next scene, Amestris prays to the Gods—"Will ye not hear, ye ever-gracious Gods?" Her prayer ends abruptly as Mirza enters, and the confrontation between the two of them rises from one act of violence to another. When Mirza forces himself upon her, Amestris pulls his own poniard from him and stabs him with it. The wound is fatal, but evil can not be so easily defeated. The guard, who appears to report the escape of Artaxerxes and Memmon, follows Mirza's order to pull Amestris to him as he lies bleeding on the floor. As his last act, Mirza stabs her as he calls her "witch; enchantress—bear thy fatal beauties down to Hell/ And try if thou canst charm among'st the dead." Lying mortally wounded, Amestris laments her fate to be thus treated just as she realizes that Artaxerxes and Memmon are alive and free.

When they enter looking for her and when Artaxerxes realizes that not only is Mirza stabbed but Amestris also, he renounces glory and bright ambition to die in her arms. Memmon, unable to bear the sight of their dying together, kills himself in his madness just as the queen enters amidst shouts and clamor from the street. Artaban, who has discovered the tragedies, would set the kingdom in order again. Content that the mob has killed Magas, he has the queen led away; and he pledges to "Let honor, truth and justice crown my reign."

II *The Literary and Political Material of the Play*

John Downes, the prompter at Lincoln's Inn Fields, assessed *The Ambitious Step-Mother* in his *Roscius Anglicanus* by stating that "the play answer'd the companies' Expectation."[2] Enacted by Betterton, Barton Booth, Mrs. Barry, and Mrs. Bracegirdle, the play enjoyed a distinguished cast for a writer's first production. Booth had been Rowe's friend at school, and the part of Artaban in Rowe's play was the first to introduce him successfully on the London stage. Downes said "'twas very well acted."[3] With the beautiful Mrs.

Bracegirdle and the accomplished Mrs. Barry in the parts of Amestris and Artemisa, respectively, and with a triangle of love, the
heroics of battle, and the drama of violence, the playgoers in the
holiday season of 1700 not surprisingly applauded Rowe's offering.

To later audiences, the play's exaggerated situations of good and
evil, love and lust, ambition and honor, contrived plot, and static
characters have made it so much of a period piece that it has seldom
been given serious consideration by the critics of eighteenth-
century drama. Compared to Dryden's or Congreve's work, this
first piece of Rowe's is indeed inferior; but, examined in its own
context as it was offered to the audience in the closing year of the
seventeenth century, it spoke their language and reflected their
interests and concerns.

In both the dedication to the printed version and twice in the
Prologue, Rowe quite directly reveals his intention of moving his
audience to pity and fear. He wished the spectator to "go away with
pity—a sort of regret proceeding from good-nature" which, "though
an uneasiness, is not altogether disgreeable to the person who feels
it. . . . this passion . . . the famous Mr. Otway succeeded so well in
touching, and must and will at all times affect people, who have any
tenderness or humanity." Rowe has obviously placed himself in the
tradition of the pathetic tragedies of Otway and Lee, and he has
accepted their definition of pity and fear. With this intention on
Rowe's part, *The Ambitious Step-Mother* becomes acceptable—
indeed, it shows clearly that in this first production Rowe intended
to move the emotions of his spectators. While his poetry may not yet
match that of Otway, his handling of detail and his denouement
precisely fit the demands of dramatic construction and the single-
ness of impression designed to appeal to the emotions of his audience.

Moreover, the whole political problem of the play was one quite
pertinent to an audience in 1700, and once again Rowe is following a
practice Otway had used successfully in his notable play *Venice
Preserved*. Like Otway, Rowe adapts several sources to construct his
own play; and, like Otway, Rowe uses violence and rhetorical means
to underscore broad and obvious moral themes. Within the serious
themes of political intrigue, presented along with music and spectacle, Rowe attempts to create the catharsis of tragedy.

Moreover, an analysis of the themes of the play shows how Rowe
has used his plot with care to achieve his purpose. Rowe's audience

probably recognized the initial situation of the play as being suggested by the biblical account of the story of David and the succession of his son Solomon,[4] for the use of biblical reference is ubiquitous in seventeenth-century literature. Indeed, the drama of the David-Absalom-Solomon situation had already been brilliantly exploited by Dryden in his *Absalom and Achitophel* in 1681; his poem only suggested the rebellion of Absalom—the Duke of Monmouth; but the rebellion did not actually take place until 1685.[5]

Rowe, writing in 1700 in a drastically changed situation since James II had abdicated the throne and fled the country, took the basic details of the problem of the succession after a popular and strong monarch and used it to show what might have happened had a tyrant and oppressor remained to command the government. Moreover, Rowe projects his consequences in the simple and universal terms of love and beauty, not in the heroic terms of honor and power. Throughout his play where a choice is to be made among honor, ambition, power, and love, Rowe has championed love. His play may have less meaning for the literary audience of the twentieth century than Dryden's poem, but its significance was apparent for the eighteenth.

Within this familiar dual reference of biblical allusion and political fable, Rowe presented his more appealing poetry of the tragedies of love. As the play opens, only the situation suggests David and his son Solomon; and Artimisa parallels Bathsheba in her beauty and in her intent to secure the throne for her son. Like David, King Arsaces is very old; like Bathsheba, Artimisa has secured the right of succession for her son in the closing hours of the old king's life. Like Bathsheba also, Artimisa has used her beauty to charm the king; like David, the king had taken her by having her husband fall in battle. There is no evidence from the biblical account of Bathsheba that she interfered with David's policy and rule as king; but Artimisa has been characterized as "heroic" in her demand for power. Unlike Bathsheba, who is encouraged by Nathan the prophet to ask David for Solomon's succession, Artimisa uses the priest Mirza for her purpose. And, unlike Bathsheba—indeed, unlike the other two "fair ladies" of the play—Artimisa is forward, grasping, and greedily ambitious. We learn, in fact, from Mirza that she quite likely schemed to have herself noticed by the king as, when he was going by in procession, he saw her beauty displayed unexpectedly when a window fell where she stood. It seems evident then that Rowe has taken from the biblical story only those details needed for his own creation and that he used the audience's familiarity with them to extend their importance—and such a procedure was the usual practice of his time.

III   *Political Implications in the Play*

When we examine the political implications of the play, we may think them to be as vague and nebulous as the biblical parallels prove to be. If, however, we realize the situation about the succession in 1700 and remember how long the problem plagued the country and upset its stability, we may find the implications of more than academic importance.[6] Mary had died childless in 1695, and William III had continued not only to maintain peace among the English people themselves but to fight a rather unpopular foreign campaign supporting his native House of Orange and opposing the spread of Louis XIV's power in Europe and in England. Throughout these closing years of William's reign, James II and his court had remained under the protection of Louis XIV; and the constant threat of the return of James always kept William apprehensive that he would not be immediately aware of the dangers against him and his government.

The kind of double intrigue used in *The Ambitious Step-Mother* was familiar to and almost of daily interest to the audience who saw Rowe's play in 1700. James II's queen, Mary of Modena, and their infant son had already fled to the safety of France that fateful Christmas season of 1688 before James himself left Whitehall. The infant son, the Prince of Wales, was immediately recognized by Louis XIV as James III and in later years was known as the "Old Pretender" who served as the focus for the Jacobites' continuing struggle to restore the House of Stuart to the throne throughout most of the eighteenth century.

In the long continuing struggle over the accession, William's health, precarious from his birth, was always a factor in political tangles both at home and abroad; and it was an even greater concern than usual in the winter of 1700. In fact, in December, when *The Ambitious Step-Mother* was produced, the king was quite ill—an illness apparent to everyone, since he was so weak that he could not walk unassisted—and his doctors had little advice to offer to make him better.[7] The other events of 1700 that added to the succession problem were the deaths in July of the little Duke of Gloucester, Anne's only child, and in November of Charles V of Spain.

Anne, Mary's younger sister, had been designated by the Act of

Succession as heir to the throne after William's death; the Duke of Gloucester was her only surviving child; and at her age, considering the fact that she had lost several children in infancy, it was not likely that she would have another.[8] The death of Charles V had long been anticipated—he was an invalid and hopelessly deranged. To one authority, Charles V had "died at the precise moment when nothing short of a World War could decide the question of his inheritance."[9] The "World War" was the War of the Spanish Succession that lasted throughout Anne's reign and beyond, for the immediate result of the death of Charles V of Spain and of the revelation of his will that was intended to keep his domains intact was that Louis XIV broke the treaty he had made with the English and their allies and that the war began in grim earnest in the early part of 1701. In summary, the topic of the problems of succession in *The Ambitious Step-Mother* was of special interest to Rowe's audience in December, 1700; it remained so for years to come.

G. M. Trevelyan, writing about this Christmas season of 1700, says that "Optimism and pacifism reigned at the festal boards of Englishmen in the Christmas of 1700. But with the New Year these sentiments received a series of rude shocks."[10] The conclusion of Rowe's play with its promise of the triumph of law and order must have been agreeable to his audience. For Rowe's admirers who read it in the early part of 1701 when it was printed, some of the intrigues and violence of the play must have seemed prophetic.[11] Moreover, the play still had significance when it was revived in 1758 when the succession was being called into question in a far different way. The cause of the Stuart Pretender had come to a final climax in 1745 when Prince Charles Edward, with the help of the French, had invaded the country; but he and his Scottish allies were soundly defeated at the battle of Culloden Moor. In 1758, then, when *The Ambitious Step-Mother* was revived, it was because the young prince, widely known to have been taught by his mother, "George, be King," was in truth about to become one. Charles Dibdin says that David Garrick did not achieve the success he had expected from his revival,[12] but this lack of appeal may be attributed to the fact that the themes of ambition and succession were no longer topical.

CHAPTER 3

Tamerlane: *A Play of Political Comment*

SO successful was Rowe's first play, *The Ambitious Step-Mother*, that he very soon produced *Tamerlane* which was so much more successful that he gained lasting recognition from it throughout most of the eighteenth century.[1] *Tamerlane* was presented by Betterton and his company at Lincoln's Inn Fields late in 1701, or early 1702; and the drama was soon published by Jacob Tonson in the first week of January, 1702. With a second edition in 1703 and a third in 1714, the play was read and discussed as well as performed. The chief reasons for its unique place in the eighteenth-century theatrical repertoire were undoubtedly its political allegory and its patriotic theme. Tamerlane, the protagonist, represents William III; Bajazet, Louis XIV. The whole of the play is a kind of pageant of good and evil in which Tamerlane represents the noble and just sentiments of a true king and in which Bajazet has the ignoble and unrestrained passions of a tyrant.

The first performance was at a time when Louis was attempting both publicly and privately to restore the throne of England to James III, whose father, James II, had died on September 13, 1701. After the resumption of the war with France in 1716, the play became a symbol of the English determination to resist until they had banished the grasping tyranny that Louis XIV represented. In the beginning of the struggle in the last decade of the seventeenth century, William had played the most important part in organizing England and her allies against Louis; and, when the Hanoverians came to the throne and restored power to the Whigs after the death of Anne in 1714, *Tamerlane* was presented each year on the fourth or fifth of November (the fourth being William's birthday anniversary and the fifth the day he landed in England) as a tribute to him and as a celebration for Whig party loyalty.

I *The Material of the Play*

As a play, *Tamerlane* exhibits no new or surprising departures
either from the established conventions of heroic tragedy or from
the characteristics of the new playwright found in *The Ambitious
Step-Mother*. In fact, it is in many ways an extension of the characterizations and themes of the earlier play. Its poetry is more elegant
and dignified than that in *The Ambitious Step-Mother*, and its action
is slighter and less confusing to follow. The play shows that Rowe is
still very much concerned with freedom, as Welwood had said; and
it shows quite clearly that his views on love and its importance make
a major theme for any dramatic situation.

In the Prologue, spoken by Betterton, Rowe suggests that he will,
like Virgil in the *Aeneid*, "tell of Fame by ancient Heroes won,"
making a pious prince his theme who "sought not fame but peace in
fields of blood." Just as Virgil used Homer, Rowe used Richard
Knolles' *Generall Historie of the Turkes*, a volume first published in
1603 and reprinted in 1687–1700, for the basis of his plot; but he
recast characters and events to suggest the themes he wished to
emphasize.[2]

The action of the play is slight and is of much less importance than
the sentiments spoken by Tamerlane and Bajazet. Tamerlane is king
of the Parthians; Bajazet, emperor of the Turks. The opening scene
before Tamerlane's tent reveals the princes who are loyal to Tamerlane anticipating the battle and predicting that

> Our Asian world
> From this important day expects a Lord,
> This day they hope an end of all their woes,
> Of tyranny, of bondage, and oppression,
> From our victorious emp'ror, *Tamerlane*. (I, 89)

In this opening scene a picture of Bajazet is also suggested, and its
details form the basis for both his character and his actions throughout the play. One of the Parthian princes reports that he has learned
from a slave who had escaped that Bajazet

> With rage redoubled, for the fight prepares;
> Some accidental passion fires his breast,
> (Love, as 'tis thought, for a fair *Grecian* captive)
> And adds new horror to his native fury:
> For five returning suns, scarce was he seen

> By any the most favour'd of his court,
> But in lascivious ease among his women,
> Liv'd from the war retir'd; or else alone
> In sullen mood sat meditating plagues,
> And ruin to the world, 'till yester morn,
> Like fire that lab'ring upwards rends the earth,
> He burst with fury from his tent, commanding
> All should be ready for the fight this day.   (I, 90)

"His sullen mood," his "lascivious ease among his women," and "his burst of fury" establish his character and mark his progress throughout the play. Moreover, we learn that he feels himself to be superior even to Heaven, for he rules

> without reason, of confounding
> Just and unjust, by an unbounded will;
> By whom religion, honour, all the bands
> That ought to hold the jarring world in peace,
> Were held the tricks of state, snares of wise Princes
> To draw their easy neighbours to destruction.   (I, 90)

His characterization, thus quite directly delineated in the opening scene, does not change even in the final scene when he himself declares, "I'll curse thee with my last, my parting breath." From the beginning, then, and throughout the play, Bajazet's actions and character serve chiefly as a foil for Rowe's Tamerlane-William tribute.

After the homage paid by the loyal princes in the introduction, Tamerlane himself appears to begin a series of passages about various topics that actually reflect the views of William III and the announced ideals of the Whigs. Significantly Tamerlane's first speech is one of regret that war "That in a moment/ Lay'st waste the noblest part of the creation" rages and "marr[s] this beauteous prospect" (I, 91). In spite of the necessities of the English position in 1701, William was indeed a man of peace; it was Louis XIV who united the loosely allied states of England, Germany, and Holland by proclaiming James III king—or rightful king of England. This act prepared the way for the victories of Blenheim and Ramillies.[3]

After the formal introduction of Tamerlane and Bajazet and after Tamerlane's own appearance when, by his words as well as his person, he "Comes like the proxy of inquiring Heav'n/ To judge and

to redress," Axalla, Tamerlane's favorite general and a Christian, is
introduced; and he appears amidst a flourish of trumpets to present
his prisoners, Monesses and Selima, Bajazet's daughter. With these
three—Axalla, Monesses, and Selima—Rowe introduces the love
theme of the play. Axalla, having fallen in love with Selima when he
was on a diplomatic mission to the court of Bajazet, introduces her
as "The noblest Prize, that ever grac'd my arms" and Monesses as
"This brave man." Monesses is a Grecian prince who has earlier
fallen into Bajazet's power along with Arpasia, his bride, whom he
has introduced as his sister. From the Axalla-Selima and the
Monesses-Arpasia love interests the complications of the sentimental subplot arise. Moreover, Axalla serves as a point upon which the
two actions of the play may converge as his success in arms and in
love prompts the jealousy of Omar, an older general to Tamerlane,
who himself would possess the beautiful Selima. The first act ends
with a tender love scene between Axalla and Selima as, just reunited, they part for Axalla to engage in battle against her father.

The outcome of the war is hardly doubtful, for Tamerlane's
triumphs are celebrated from the beginning. Moreover, the contrast
of Tamerlane with Bajazet dominates the action. The captive
Monesses reports the conclusion of the battle as he turns his
thoughts to Arpasia only to discover that Bajazet has not only held
her captive but also forced her into marriage with him. Hardly has
Bajazet's cruelty been described when he and his generals are
brought in chains before Tamerlane. As Tamerlane receives him, he
deplores the necessity of war, declaring to Bajazet:

> When I survey the ruins of this field,
> The wild destruction, which thy fierce ambition
> Has dealt among mankind (so many widows
> And helpless orphans has thy battle made,
> That half our Eastern world this day are mourners)
> Well may I, in behalf of Heav'n and Earth,
> Demand from thee atonement for this wrong. (I, 104)

In his turn, Bajazet will neither admit guilt nor sue for mercy; for
he replies:

> Make thy demand to those that own thy pow'r,
> Know, I am still beyond it; and tho fortune
> (Curse on that changeling Diety of fools)

> Has stript me of the train and pomps of greatness
> That out-side of a King, yet still my soul,
> Fixt high, and of itself alone dependent
> Is ever free and royal, and ev'n now
> As at the head of battle does defy thee: (I, 104–105)

His chains unbound by Tamerlane's orders, Bajazet continues his ranting as he replies to Tamerlane's offer of peace with honor:

> Damnation on thee! thou smooth fawning talker!
> Give me again my chains, that I may curse thee,
> And gratify my rage: Or, if thou wilt
> Be a vain fool, and play with thy perdition,
> Remember I'm thy foe, and hate thee deadly.   (I, 105)

Only as the second act ends is the complication of love resumed when Monesses realizes the full extent of Bajazet's villainy. Arpasia, graciously returned by Tamerlane, who is ignorant of her true relationship to Monesses, is spurned by Bajazet and left to unfold her tale of sorrow to her true husband, Monesses, in moving speeches of passionate desperation. Ruined by Bajazet, she feels she can no longer be possessed by Monesses and can find peace only in death. Overcome by his loss and her sorrow, Monesses ends the fearful dialogue by begging her to sustain his failing faith as he joins her in wishing for death.

In acts III and IV, Rowe develops the love complications and introduces the themes of rebellion and religious fanaticism. Axalla is refused the hand of Selima by her father, Bajazet; moreover, Tamerlane discovers the true situation of Arpasia and Monesses. To the sorrows of unrequited loves are added the dangers of rebellion. Tamerlane is threatened by a Dervish who demands the dismissal of the Christian Axalla; Tamerlane, unafraid of him, defies him; and, even as the Dervish offers to kill him, Tamerlane sends him away without punishment. Meantime, Bajazet has discovered that Omar, one of Tamerlane's oldest and most trusted generals, has become violently jealous of Axalla's place as favorite and would not only deprive him of his honors but also rob him of Selima. The three— Bajazet, Omar, and the Dervish—plot together to destroy Tamerlane in order to accomplish their own evil ends. Bajazet offers the hand of his daughter Selima to Omar as they plan to destroy Tamerlane and satisfy their own ambitions.

But such destruction is not possible; evil can destroy the innocent but not the power of the righteous. When Bajazet comes upon Tamerlane alone with Arpasia and would accuse them of adultery, Tamerlane's resolution to maintain justice and magnanimity cannot be shaken, although at this point, where honor is the contest, he comes very near to losing his self-control. He is saved by the pleas of the beautiful and pathetic Arpasia, who begs him to "Call back the doom of death" he has in his anger imposed on Bajazet. Yielding to her, Tamerlane agrees, but Bajazet, furious to receive Tamerlane's reprieve through her request, repays her "precious pray'rs" with the full force of his anger when, in the plot to overthrow Tamerlane, Monesses falls into his power. Bajazet has Monesses killed before Arpasia's very eyes in spite of her former mercy to him and her now impassioned cry for him to spare Monesses. Failing to move him, Arpasia sinks to the floor in death just as Monesses is strangled.

Such evil cannot go unpunished. Tamerlane, Axalla, and their friends, having discovered the attempted rebellion, rush in to save Selima from her wicked father and to give her to Axalla rather than honor her father's pledge of her to Omar. Bajazet is imprisoned in a cage to serve as a visible example for all who would forget that pride is the deadliest of The Seven Deadly Sins. Act V, and the play, ends with Tamerlane's concluding observations:

> Behold the vain effects of earth-born pride,
> That scorn'd Heav'n's laws, and all its pow'r defied:
> That could the hand, which form'd it first, forget,
> And fondly say, I made myself be great:
> But justly those above assert their sway,
> And teach ev'n Kings what homage they should pay,
> Who then rule best, when mindful to obey.   (I, 149)

If the plot of *Tamerlane* is slight and if its situations are the conventional ones of conflict between great rulers, rebellion among the nobility, and the tragedies of unrequited love, the characters are archetypal. As the epic hero, Tamerlane is portrayed in exaggerated outlines; and, as his protagonist, Bajazet is even more imposing. Rowe has chosen to delineate their characters with words rather than with actions. With such an initial choice, he could do little more than present a series of homilies in developing the progression of the play.

II *The Political Homilies of the Play*

The political implications of the play are made evident from the
beginning. Tamerlane's first speech about the "wild destruction" of
war is followed by a series of speeches addressed to Selima and
Monesses—to Selima, to show his appreciation of innocence and
beauty; to Monesses, to show his understanding that valor and brav-
ery may be found among his enemies. In all of Tamerlane's speeches
in the first act, we find the repeated theme of freedom: freedom
from war that brings peace, freedom from the tyranny of a wicked
ruler that brings the happiness of personal choice. Tyranny has no
place except as it becomes the tyranny of the fair, and even then, as
Axalla says to Selima,

> Hear, sweet Heav'n
> Hear the fair tyrant, how she wrests love's laws,
> As she had vow'd my ruin! What is conquest?
> What joy have I from that, but to behold thee,
> To kneel before thee, and with lifted eyes
> To view thee, as devotion does a saint,
> With awful, trembling pleasure: (I, 97–98)

The only desirable tyranny is that of the gods and saints. In this
world of reality, the cause of freedom must be defended by the
strong—by such a hero as Tamerlane; for no less a hero will suffice.

The contrast to Tamerlane and his attitudes is sharply and surely
drawn in Bajazet's speeches, ones repeated throughout the play, on
the theme of power that is centered in the self-directed exultation of
pride as it is exemplified by such a tyrant as Bajazet; no less than the
tyrant himself will reveal the excellences of the hero, Tamerlane.
Bajazet's first speech, revealing his defiance of Tamerlane and all he
represents, is delivered as he is brought on stage in chains, a prisoner of war. He refuses to admit that he has been conquered; he
argues that he has only been deprived of the "train and pomps of
greatness" by "fortune . . . that changeling Deity of fools!" His
impassioned speech pleads the liberty of the mind, but a mind held
captive by its passions. Reason, talk—the servant of Reason ("the
friendly parle of neighbouring Princes met")—Bajazet rejects. He
taunts Tamerlane by calling him "Thou Pedant Talker": "This vile
speeching,/ This after fame of words, is what most irks me;/ Spare
that, and for the rest, 'tis equal all—/ Be it as it may" (I, 105).

For Bajazet, a king and ambition make an equal equation; and
hate and destruction are necessary steps to establish such a formula
for the control of an empire and ultimately. for immortality itself.
Ambition is "The noble appetite which will be satisfy'd,/ And like
the food of Gods, make him immortal." To Bajazet's vaunting,
Tamerlane replies:

> Henceforth I will not wonder we were foes,
> Since souls that differ so, by nature hate,
> And strong antipathy forbids their union.
> *Baj.* The noble fire that warms me does indeed
> transcend thy coldness; I am pleas'e we differ,
> Nor think alike.
> *Tam.* No—for I think like man,
> Thou like a monster; from whose baleful presence
> Nature starts back;   (I, 105)

It is certainly in the ideas of these speeches that the eighteenth
century found *Tamerlane* a suitable tribute not only to William III
but also to the establishment of the Whigs. As the speeches between
Tamerlane and Bajazet continue, one after another of the great
Whig principles is set forth. On the subject of kingship, Tamerlane
voices William's moderate views:

> 'Tis true, I am a King, as thou hast been:
> Honour, and glory too have been my aim;
> But tho' I dare face death, and all the dangers,
> Which furious war wears in its bloody front,
> Yet would I chuse to fix my name by peace,
> By justice, and mercy; and to raise
> My trophies on the blessings of mankind;
> Nor would I buy the empire of the world
> With ruin of the people whom I sway,
> On forfeit of my honour.   (I, 106)

Bajazet calls him a "tame King," a "preaching Dervise"

> Unfit for war, thou shouldst have liv'd secure
> In lazy peace, and with debating senates
> Shar'd a precarious scepter, sat tamely still,
> And let bold factions canton out thy pow'r
> And wrangle for the spoils they robb'd thee of;

> Whilst I (curse on the pow'r that stops my ardour!)
> Would, like a tempest, rush amidst the nations,
> Be greatly terrible, and deal, like *Alba*,
> My angry thunder on the frighted world.   (I, 106)

Indeed, Tamerlane replies that the world is too small for such pride as Bajazet displays; that, in fact, he would scale Heaven itself. To which Bajazet agrees:

> I would:—Away! my soul
> Disdains thy conference.
> *Tam.* Thou vain, rash thing,
> That, with gigantic insolence, hast dar'd
> To lift thy wretched self above the stars,
> And mate with pow'r almighty: Thou art fall'n!
> *Baj.* 'Tis false! I am not fall'n from ought I've been:
> At least my soul resolves to keep her state,
> And scorns to take acquaintance with ill fortune.
> *Tam.* Almost beneath my pity art thou fall'n
> Since, while th' avenging hand of Heav'n is on thee,
> And presses to the dust thy swelling soul,
> Fool-hardy, with the stronger thou contendest;
> To what vast heights had thy tumultuous temper
> Been hurry'd, if success had crown'd thy wishes;
> Say, what had I to expect, if thou had'st conquer'd?   (I, 106)

In reply to Tamerlane's question, Bajazet makes clear that he has no mercy, that his only action would be to raise himself on the ruins of others. To Tamerlane he says:

> I had us'd thee, as thou art to me,—a dog,
> The object of my scorn, and mortal hatred:
> I would have taught thy neck to know my weight,
> And mounted from that footstool to my saddle;
> Then, when thy daily servile task was done,
> I would have cag'd thee, for the scorn of slaves,
> Till thou hadst begg'd to die; and ev'n that mercy
> I had deny'd thee: (I, 107)

In contrast to the words of the tyrant, Tamerlane suggests that, if he could, he would wish for Bajazet that

>   thou forget thy brutal fierceness,
> And form thyself to manhood, I would bid thee,
> Live, and be still a King, that thou may'st learn
> What man should be to man, in war rememb'ring
> The common tye, and brotherhood of kind.   (I, 107)

And, as a final conclusion to the discussion of war, kingship, tyranny, justice, mercy, and the brotherhood of mankind, Tamerlane speaks of virtue:

>   Virtue still does
> With scorn the mercenary world regard,
> Where abject souls do good, and hope reward:
> Above the worthless trophies men can raise,
> She seeks not honours, wealth, nor airy praise,
> But with herself, herself, the goddess pays.   (I, 108)

In Tamerlane's refusal to command Bajazet's death and in the generous and courteous way Bajazet is treated, an additional contrast between the two is revealed. In his sumptuous royal tent, with his servants about him, his beautiful wife restored, Bajazet is confounded with kindness. Tamerlane is indeed willing to support his words by deeds; as king and man, he can do no more. Indeed, as the action of the play progresses, Rowe uses several incidents to emphasize the admirable personal qualities of Tamerlane and the unfeeling selfishness of Bajazet. Tamerlane's cool courage in defending himself from the Dervish intensifies the audience's sympathy for him, while Bajazet's refusal to recognize Axalla's worth, as well as his demand that Axalla must bring him the head of Tamerlane in exchange for the hand of Selima, confirms our judgment that Bajazet is, as Tamerlane has said, a kind of monster. Moreover, the demand for Tamerlane's head places Bajazet with Herod as the wicked, lascivious ruler who would destroy both the prophet and his Master. The allusion is quite clear; the only difference between Bajazet and Herod is one of time, for they are equally vicious. Selima, however, unlike Herod's daughter, refuses to aid her father: she falters only briefly because of her filial devotion to him. In the end, she secretly releases Axalla, who in turn warns Tamerlane and thus brings about Bajazet's final disgrace as the plan that Omar suggested and that Bajazet attempted fails.

On a second and only slightly less important level, Bajazet's cruel and ruthless treatment of Arpasia and Selima reinforce our view of him as a cruel tyrant. He forces his will on them arbitrarily; not once does he allow either Arpasia or Selima any choice. The only human touch Bajazet possesses is his regard for his daughter, but so slight is his feeling that the only time she crosses him, he is ready to kill her and she has to be rescued by Tamerlane and Axalla. Bajazet's treatment of Arpasia is even more inhumane; for, while there may be some justification for his anger with Selima who frustrated his attempt to regain power, his treatment of Arpasia is totally dishonorable. Earlier he had captured her along with Monesses, her bridegroom, when, having broken his word, he had invaded Greece and taken it by force before this battle with Tamerlane. Then, in spite of Arpasia's impassioned pleas, he had his own priest say a false ceremony of marriage; and he had forcibly consummated that marriage over the protests of the helpless Arpasia. The false ceremony itself serves as an ironic parallel to the previous one between Monesses and Arpasia which, true and right in every aspect, had, nevertheless, remained unconsummated. In both negative and positive ways, the tyrant Bajazet attempts to destroy both honor and love. He himself is impervious to both, but he can destroy neither in Arpasia.

Reunited with Monesses, Arpasia shows her impassioned love for him and her precise and dramatic sense of honor; but she refuses to hope for joy with him when she says:

> And who shall render back my peace, my honour,
> The spotless whiteness of my virgin soul?
> Ah! no, *Monesses*—think not I will ever
> Bring a polluted love to thy chaste arms:
> I am the tyrant's wife, Oh, fatal title!
> And, in the sight of all the saints, have sworn,
> By honour, womanhood, and blushing shame,
> To know no second bride-bed but my grave. (I, 112)

Moreover, her virtue and purity become a real force in the action of the play. Her careful sense of honor is revealed again when she pleads for Bajazet's life when Tamerlane, angry with Bajazet's accusation that Tamerlane has come for "amorous parley" with her, loses his control and orders a guard to "Seize and drag him to his fate." Arpasia will not allow Bajazet's false honor to disturb the purity of Tamerlane's.

Tamerlane's own action and speech in the context of the love scenes are added proof of his magnanimity. But his words to Arpasia—"Oh matchless virtue! Yes, I will obey; . . . / I will pursue the shining path thou tred'st . . . / Wisely from dangerous passions I retreat "(I, 134)—suggest a far more pervasive concern with love and honor than the immediate action of the play. Tamerlane is certainly developed as the ideal ruler whose sensibilities enable him to understand the whole range of human response. Bajazet's suggestion that he spoke with Arpasia in "amorous parley" is as insulting to Tamerlane's virtue as it is to hers. Indeed, Tamerlane's virtue is equal to that of Arpasia; the incident in which it is questioned is the only provocation in the play that causes Tamerlane to lose control of his temper and to allow his passions, not his reason, to dictate his words. To have been less responsive would have made him less ideal. In the conclusion of the scene, Arpasia brings him back to reason; and, by this return to reason, he maintains his power. In both reason and sensibility, then, Tamerlane is the image of the ideal ruler.

III   *The Theme of Love*

Tamerlane's tender regard for Arpasia and the importance of love as a part of the action of the play show that Rowe equated the ideal ruler with both power and compassion. Love, the evil of uncontrolled passions, and the power of beauty are all themes in Rowe's view of tragedy; but Rowe's use of them in *Tamerlane* is much more skillfully handled than in *The Ambitious Step-Mother*. From the beginning of *Tamerlane*, the twin threads of war and peace, love and happiness, are managed in such a way that we cannot make one design without the other; and such a tightly woven design is not evident in *The Ambitious Step-Mother*. In this earlier play, Rowe's handling of the complications of love had been almost that of theme and variation as he showed the tragic triangle of young love in Artaxerxes, Amestris, and the pathetic Cleone as it developed against the foil of the evil queen, Artemisa; her licentious minister, Mirza; and the grasping high priest, Magas.

There are, of course, similarities in the two plays; and the most striking ones are in the drama of the destruction of innocence and virtue brought about by the uncontrolled power of Mirza in *The*

Ambitious Step-Mother and of Bajazet in *Tamerlane*. But even in these instances important differences exist. The improbable action of the rape scene in *The Ambitious Step-Mother* has become the forced marriage of Bajazet and Arpasia in *Tamerlane*. The melodramatic deaths of Amestris and Artaxerxes in *The Ambitious Step-Mother* become the much less bloody strangulation of Monesses. Arpasia, seeing Monesses die, succumbs to grief and fear: her death then is much more pathetic than violent.

Moreover, Rowe has taken another step toward a realistic handling of the lovers and the situation of love in *Tamerlane*. Indeed, the responses of the lovers to their situations are more natural than those in *The Ambitious Step-Mother*. Axalla, for all his great love of Selima, acts his proper part as friend and favorite of Tamerlane. His role in the scene with Selima—when, after having been reunited, they must part for him to do battle with her father—is a nicely conceived one; and their final happiness is much more reasonable than the somewhat uncertainly prepared for denouement of *The Ambitious Step-Mother* where Amestris, staggering back on the stage after being stabbed by the dying Mirza, prompts Artaxerxes to stab himself and her father to go mad.

Another notable feature of the love theme in *Tamerlane* is Rowe's care in presenting the sanctity of marriage. In *The Ambitious Step-Mother*, Artaxerxes and Amestris are taken prisoner almost immediately after the sacred ceremony that had united them; and Amestris is taken away at once by Mirza with no time for the marriage to be consummated. She escapes being raped only by stabbing Mirza and is reunited with her husband, Artaxerxes, only in the final moments before they die. In *Tamerlane*, when we first see Arpasia and Monesses brought together, tragedy has already been imposed upon them. Since Monesses' separation from her, Arpasia has been forced into a false and hideous marriage with Bajazet; consequently, her relationship with Monesses must be drastically different. She has in fact been raped—no matter the hollow ceremony by Bajazet's spurious priest—and the sanctity of marriage must now be that of love denied.

In the situation of the other couple of the play, Axalla and Selima, Rowe again touches upon the question of how much and what kind of authority a parent might exercise in an arranged marriage. Bajazet rejects Axalla as not being of proper birth for Selima; instead, he offers her to Omar in exchange for Omar's treachery. The obvious use of the beautiful Selima in such a way confirms our view of Bajazet just as Mirza's cruel treatment of Amestris shows the inevitable conclusion of passion and lust. In the closing scene of *Tamerlane*, even at the point where Selima expects to be stabbed in accordance with her father's commands, she asks leave for a moment "while I pray,/ That Heaven may guard my Royal Father." Her dramatic salvation by Axalla and Tamerlane is yet another justice done to such proper filial devotion. The conclusion of the theme of love and the lovers is made then in terms of the strength and security of Tamerlane and his just use of power as he helps rescue Selima and, in doing so, reaffirms his power over the tyranny of Bajazet, her father. Rowe has brought together neatly his themes of power and greatness, of honor and love.

IV *The Pageantry of the Play*

Although we have discussed two of the important reasons for the success and continued popularity of *Tamerlane*, a third characteristic of the play made it a memorable vehicle for patriotic celebration; Rowe's epic intentions make a suitable form for the pageantry and the rhetoric that made the play appropriate for its annual presentation. In the stage setting, as well as in the action, the audience was reminded that it was designed for a significance beyond its plot. In making its setting the exotic battlefields of Persia, Rowe is following the conventions of the heroic plays which were usually set in such far places; but the rich pageantry of the opening scene with Tamerlane's tent in the background and the invocation offered by the Prince of Tanais suggest at once that the ceremony and pomp on the stage will contribute to the compliment paid in making Tamerlane shadow forth William III. The traditional sun image is used; the flourish of trumpets announces Tamerlane's entrance; Axalla kneels as he offers Tamerlane his prisoners—all details that create the proper mood in the very beginning of the play; and the ceremonies and manners associated with the court and Tamerlane's dignified, somewhat formal speech maintain these characteristics throughout. The use of music as background adds an important feature, and the interpolation of a song between the plotting of Bajazet and Omar and the sad lament of Arpasia on her fate marks a sharp contrast indeed—the kind of contrast suitable not for drama but for pageantry. With the combination then of dramatic action, heroic characters, and epic themes, *Tamerlane* provided the acceptable means for an annual celebration of liberty, justice, and compassion triumphant over tyranny, injustice, and hate.

V *The History of* Tamerlane

The stage history of *Tamerlane* and the shifting critical evaluation of the play read like a chapter in the history of eighteenth-century drama. Downes says the play was "in general well acted; but chiefly the parts of Mr. Betterton, Verbuggen, Mr. Powel, Madam Bracegirdle and Barry: which made it a stock play."[4] Betterton was Tamerlane; Verbruggen, Bajazet; as Selima, the beautiful Mrs. Bracegirdle must have been perfectly cast; and Mrs. Barry as Arpasia must have fit precisely the comment Colley Cibber made of her when he said that, "in the Art of exciting Pity, she had a Power beyond all other Actresses I have yet seen, or what your Imagination can conceive."[5]

Successful upon its initial presentation, *Tamerlane* acquired a kind of enduring fame when the "parties" realized its value as a political comment. After the Treaty of Utrecht, the play was not given for a while since the portrait of Louis XIV was such a severe one; but, since the peace did not last, the play was soon used again as political propaganda.[6] In 1716, a notable revival was ordered by the Lord Chamberlain "which was got up with the utmost magnificence."[7]

In the twentieth century, the identification of the characters has engaged the attention of several scholars. As early as 1710, Charles Gildon suggested that Rowe had a "double Object in view when he writ it" and that most of his characters "are assimilated to some Great Persons now living."[8] James Sutherland identifies Axalla as Prince Eugene and Omar as the Earl of Danby;[9] Willard Thorpe identifies Axalla with Hans William Bentick, the first Earl of Portland,[10] an identification that seems to fit more exactly than the identification of Axalla with Danby. Whatever the specific identifications may be, the fact is that William III's fear of rebellion was very real. Indeed, one of the reasons for the long interest in the ideas of *Tamerlane* is certainly that the problem of the succession and of the Jacobites' plans for the return of the direct heirs of James II continued for so long into the century. In December, 1701, not three months after the death of James II, these plans were very much feared and discussed.

A review of such dramatic events reveals clearly Rowe's intention of theme. It may be observed that again the qualities of heroic drama and Rowe's own adaptation of them combine to reveal the theme; and both are skillfully handled. As Eugene Waith says, "Tamerlane has 'No Lust for Rule.'"[11] Rowe has made him the ideal ruler in every circumstance and situation, and it is not surprising that the play remained such powerful political propaganda for so long a time.

CHAPTER 4

The Fair Penitent:
"A melancholy tale of private woes"

ROWE'S third play, *The Fair Penitent*, was produced at Lincoln's Inn Fields in May, 1703. Downes's judgment of it was: "A very good play for three Acts: but failing in the two last, it answer'd not their Expectation."[1] Its later popularity makes such a statement rather puzzling. Perhaps one of the reasons "it answer'd not their Expectation" was the ludicrous incident said to have occurred on opening night during the solemn death-watch scene at the beginning of Act V when the servant who was the corpse cried aloud, stood up, ran from the stage, and caused the audience to be convulsed with laughter.[2] In any case, the play was relatively well received during its first run; thereafter, this tragedy in blank verse appeared throughout the eighteenth and far into the nineteenth century.

As a play, *The Fair Penitent* was the first of Rowe's "she-tragedies" and, in the words of one of its later critics, "a landmark in eighteenth-century drama."[3] Rowe's source for the plot was Philip Massinger and Nathan Field's *The Fatal Dowry*, but his use of Massinger and Field makes *The Fair Penitent* quite another play; and, if the source's forceful romanticism is lost in Rowe, its rough judgment is also absent.[4] The characters of *The Fatal Dowry* were transformed by Rowe into eighteenth-century ladies and gentlemen, and he compressed the events of *The Fatal Dowry*, changed the emphasis of the theme of repentance, and recast the characters to his own design.[5]

I *The Action and Questions of the Play*

The plot of *The Fair Penitent* is somewhat uncertain in places, perhaps because Rowe had difficulty in reworking the already con-

fused narrative of *The Fatal Dowry*. Rowe's play opens with a
dialogue between Altamont, the protagonist, and his friend Horatio.
It is Altamont's wedding day, upon which he will be united with
Calista, the daughter of his patron and benefactor, Sciolto. This
opening scene is rather awkward in that Rowe's attempt to compress
the whole first act of *The Fatal Dowry* becomes tedious because of
the detail it must report, but the facts revealed are essential to our
understanding the play. From the conversation, we learn that Sciolto became Altamont's friend when Altamont had experienced
poverty and despair after the death of his father. Horatio reminds
Altamont that Sciolto had raised him "half dead and drooping o'er
thy father's grave" and had restored to him the "high rank and
lustre" that he had lost when his father had been ruined by the
ungrateful Genoa senate who had "made their court to faction."

Sciolto not only had saved Altamont from public ruin but in his
love for him had promised him the hand of Calista, his beautiful
daughter. So magnanimous indeed is Sciolto that he has even included in his bounty Horatio who is married to Altamont's sister,
Lavinia. Sciolto, who appears as Horatio and Altamont converse
with each other, repeats all his promises; but, in spite of his pros-
pects, Altamont is depressed because he has found Calista to be as
"cold as a dead lover's statue on his tomb." As the men speak
together about "the virgin bride," her betrayer, Lothario, appears
and speaks arrogantly to his friend Rossano about his "triumph o'er
Calista." Members of Lothario's family are deadly enemies of Altamont; indeed, they were largely responsible for his father's disgrace and death. From the dialogue between Rossano and Lothario,
we learn that Lothario has already made a mockery of the wedding
day and that he plans to use his triumph over Calista for his own
selfish purposes. When Rossano says, "You lov'd her once,"
Lothario replies,

> I lik'd her, wou'd have married her,
> But that it pleas'd her father to refuse me,
> To make this honourable fool her husband.
> For which, if I forget him, may the shame
> I mean to brand his name with, stick on mine.   (I, 161)

As they continue their conversation, Calista's situation becomes
tragically clear. Lothario says that she "oft in private gave me hear-

ing,/ 'Till by long list'ning to the soothing tale,/ At length her easy heart was wholly mine." Rossano's wonder that "virtue thus defended, should be yielded / A prey to loose desires" elicits a moving description of Calista's fall from innocence. Lothario says:

> Here then, I'll tell thee.
> Once in a lone and secret hour of night,
> When ev'ry eye was clos'd, and the pale moon
> And stars alone, shone conscious of the theft,
> Hot with the *Tuscan* grape, and high in blood,
> Hap'ly I stole unheeded to her chamber.
> . . . .
> I found the fond, believing, love-sick maid,
> Loose, unattir'd, warm, tender, full of wishes:
> Fierceness and pride, the guardians of her
>   honor,
> Were charm'd to rest, and love alone was
>   waking.
> . . . .
> I snatch'd the glorious, golden opportunity,
> And with prevailing, youthful ardor prest her,
> Till with short sighs, and murmuring
>   reluctance,
> The yielding fair one gave me perfect happi-
>   ness.
> Ev'n all the live-long night we pass'd in bliss,
> In ecstasies too fierce to last for ever;
> At length the morn and cold indiff'rence came;
> When fully sated with the luscious banquet,
> I hastily took leave, and left the nymph
> To think on what was past, and sigh alone.
>   (I, 161–62)

Having enjoyed Calista, Lothario's ardor cooled—"reason took her turn to reign"—and Calista "With uneasy fondness . . . hung upon me, wept, and sigh'd and swore/ She was undone; talk'd of a priest, and marriage." Lothario "Escap'd the persecution," for he resolved to have "love·and peace of mind" and "never to load it with the marriage-chain" that means "ill-nature, cares, and quarrels" (I, 162–63). After Lothario's account of the situation, we are ready to offer our sympathy to Calista, whatever her actions may be or have been.

But Calista does not yet appear; and, before she does so in the
second act, our sympathy for her has been additionally aroused
when Lothario encounters her maid, Lucilla; for, in the ensuing
scene, we learn more about his perfidy. About her mistress Lucilla
reports that

> By day she seeks some melancholy shade,
> To hide her sorrows from the prying world;
> At night she watches all the long long hours,
> And listens to the winds and beating rain,
> And sighs as loud, and tears that fall as fast,
> And cries, false! false! *Lothario!*   (I, 164)

Unmoved by the touching picture of Calista's sorrow, Lothario
speaks insolently:

> Oh, no more!
> I swear thou'lt spoil thy pretty face with crying,
> And thou hast beauty that may make thy fortune;
> Some keeping cardinal shall dote upon thee,
> And barter his Church treasure for thy freshness.   (I, 164)

Lucilla's reply to such insolence reflects the views of many a fair
member of Rowe's audience:

> What! shall I sell my innocence and youth,
> For wealth or titles, to perfidious man!
> To man! who makes his mirth of our undoing?
> The base, profest betrayer of our sex!
> Let me grow old in all misfortunes else,
> Rather than know the sorrows of *Calista*.   (I, 164)

When Lucilla gives him Calista's letter, it prompts Lothario to call
Calista "the fair inconstant" because he has read that her hand has
already been given to Altamont; and his careless loss of the letter as
he flees the garden extends Calista's tragedy to all those who love
her—to Altamont and her father and ultimately to Horatio and
Lavinia. When Horatio, entering the garden and finding the letter,
reads it, he immediately realizes that the true situation of the
tragedy reaches far beyond that of "the lost *Calista*." His thoughts
turn first to his friend Altamont, "the wretched husband," who is

perhaps even now gazing "fondly on her,/ And thinking soul and
body both alike,/ Blesses the perfect workmanship of Heav'n." As
for Calista's father, his "justice dooms her dead, / And [it] breaks his
heart with sorrow; . . ." (I, 166). Horatio's moving speech picturing
Altamont's happiness and Sciolto's goodness makes quite dramatic
the ramifications of Calista's act; and Horatio as guardian of her
secret is placed at the center of the tragedy.

In the last scene of the first act, Rowe characterizes the virtuous
wife when Lavinia appears while Horatio stands debating the decision he must make about the letter he has found. Lavinia's character
and her role in the play add depth to Calista's plight. As Horatio's
wife and as Altamont's sister, she is both the ideal wife and the
understanding friend. Horatio refuses to burden her with his sorrow, but he ends the scene with a tribute to her:

> Oh, were they all like thee men would adore 'em,
> And all the bus'ness of their lives be loving;
> The nuptial band shou'd be the pledge of peace,
> And all domestic cares and quarrels cease;
> The world should learn to love by virtuous rules,
> And marriage be no more the jest of fools.　(I, 168)

With the introduction of Lavinia, Rowe suggests the rules of the
virtuous. Calista is to be pitied even more as she is contrasted to
Lavinia.

The second act opens with a scene between Calista and Lucilla. In
this first appearance of Calista, her emotional and psychological
state is made immediately clear: she vacillates between a desire to
withdraw from the world and a passionate drive to continue her role
as Lothario's mistress. From her first conversation, we realize that
she is not now—nor ever will be—repentant. Hers is no dissenter's
tale of guilt, sorrow, and forgiveness to save her soul from hell if not
to save her life from the law. In her first speech she says, "For oh!
I've gone around through all my thoughts,/ But all are indignation,
love or shame,/ And my dear peace of mind is lost for ever." Lucilla
chides her and says what is obviously true,

> Why do you follow still that wand'ring fire,
> That has mis-led your weary steps, and leaves you
> Benighted in a wilderness of woe?
> That false *Lothario!*　(I, 169)

Calista will not accept such advice. She would first flee to some "dismal melancholy Scene"; and, then reminded of the real world, she speaks with scorn "Of each affected she that tells my story,/ And blesses her good stars that she is virtuous" (I, 169). Lucilla, frightened at Calista's undisciplined emotional outburst, warns her:

> Can you perceive the manifest destruction,
> The gaping gulf that opens just before you,
> And yet rush on, tho' conscious of the danger?
> . . . .
> My trembling heart forebodes, let me intreat you,
> Never to see this faithless man again: (I, 170)

But Calista, overcome with passion, declares, "On thy life/ I charge thee no; my genius drives me on;/ I must, I will behold him once again" (I, 170). Lucilla, after hearing such an unbridled emotional outburst, prays that she may be guarded from men: "From their deceitful tongues, their vows and flatteries. . . . Let my bloom wither, and my form decay,/ That none may think it worth his while to ruin me,/ And fatal love may never be my bane" (I, 170). Such a simple solution can never be that of either Calista or Altamont, however.

Even as Calista and Lucilla converse, Altamont comes to claim his bride; and she, predicting woe to all of them, goes reluctantly with him. On this note of foreboding gloom, the entertainment of music and dancing is introduced to celebrate the wedding. Sciolto makes a speech of welcome and a toast to the bride and the groom. The festivities completed, all the company leave except Horatio, who remains ridden with uncertainty; he cannot forget the fateful letter. Immediately following the strange wedding scene, Horatio goes into the street, where he encounters Lothario and his friend Rossano. He confronts them, telling them of finding the letter and accusing them of forging it. If Lothario represented the unrepentant rake in his first appearance, he now shows his qualities of gallantry. Fearless, haughty, and proud, Lothario boasts about his name and offers to draw his sword. Rossano restrains him while Horatio continues to accuse them of plotting to slander Calista's honor. Horatio cannot believe that any noble lady—certainly not Calista—can willingly fall victim to the gallant's trick, can yield herself as completely to him as the evidence in the letter clearly indicates she has done. As they argue, Horatio says:

> Away! no woman could descend so low:
> A skipping, dancing, worthless tribe you are,
> Fit only for yourselves: You herd together;
> And when the circling glass warms your vain hearts,
> You talk of beauties that you never knew.   (I, 175)

Lothario in his arrogance will not deign to answer until, finally wearied of Horatio's sermons, he makes quite clear his own views when he says,

> By the joys,
> Which my soul has uncontroll'd pursu'd
> I would not turn aside from my least pleasure,
> Tho' all thy force were arm'd to bar my ways;
> But like the birds, great nature's happy commoners,
> That haunt in woods, in meads, and flow'ry gardens,
> Rifle the sweets, and taste the choicest fruits,
> Yet scorn to ask the lordly owner's leave.   (I, 176)

Moreover, he refuses to be detained "By a dependent on the wretched Altamont,/ A talking Sir, that brawls for him in taverns, And vouches for his valor's reputation." Rossano again separates the two, and they part reluctantly only after agreeing to fulfill their code of honor by meeting for a duel.

Lothario may be a villain, but Horatio is a self-righteous coxcomb in this confrontation. From the dialogue, we may easily see why Lothario won the hearts of the females in the audience. His bold sophistication, his independent arrogance, and his satanic charm make him as attractive as Horatio is unattractive. Horatio's strictly moral preachments make him pompous. Since the audience already knows the true situation, Horatio's comments condemn Calista quite as much as they do Lothario—more, in fact, since Lothario's sophisticated view is certainly as tolerated as Horatio's. Left alone on the stage, Horatio ends the second act with a sentimental speech that condemns not only Çalista but all women, since few of them would agree with his pious cant. Horatio has believed Lothario without giving Calista any opportunity to defend herself in any way. She, along with all other women, is accused categorically as Horatio declaims:

> . . . Oh unthinking fool—
> What if I urg'd her with the crime and danger?

If any spark from Heav'n remain unquenched
Within her breast, my breath perhaps may wake it;
Could I but prosper there, I would not doubt
My combat with that loud vain-glorious boaster.
Were you, ye fair, but cautious whom ye trust,
Did you but think how seldom fools are just,
So many of your sex would not in vain,
Of broken vows, and faithless men, complain.
Of all the various wretches love has made,
How few have been by men of sense betrayed?
Convinc'd by reason, they your pow'r confess,
Pleas'd to be happy, as you're pleas'd to bless.
And conscious of your worth, can never love you less. (I 177–78)

But who would agree to be cautious in Lothario's presence, or to choose a man of sense who had been convinc'd by reason? Out of context, Lothario's position may indeed be indefensible and Horatio's admirably moral; but in the context of the play—of Calista's situation—Horatio is simply dull. Both within the development of the plot and in the criticism that appeared almost simultaneously with the play, Lothario's ambivalent charms have been frequently analyzed and as frequently condemned.

As if Calista's position were not difficult enough, Act III begins with a harsh confrontation between Calista and her father. In spite of Sciolto's kindness and consideration for Altamont, Horatio, and Lavinia, his conduct to his daughter is hardly acceptable to those sympathetic with her dilemma. He cannot understand her reluctance to accept his choice, Altamont. When her father departs, Calista, left alone, speaks sentiments that must have been representative in some degree of most of the women who listened:

How hard is the condition of our sex,
Thro' ev'ry state of life the slaves of man?
In all the dear delightful days of youth,
A rigid father dictates to our wills,
And deals out pleasure with a scanty hand:
To his, the tyrant husband's reign succeeds;
Proud with opinion of superior reason,
He holds domestic bus'ness and devotion
All we are capable to know, and shuts us,
Like cloister'd idiots, from the world's acquaintance,
And all the joys of freedom. Wherefore are we
Born with high souls, but to assert ourselves,

> Shake off this vile obedience they exact,
> And claim an equal empire o'er the world?   (I, 179)

As she finishes her declaration of independence, Horatio enters with an offer to support her grief. She will have none of his intrusion as she replies "To steal unlooked for on my private sorrow,/ Speaks not the man of honour, nor the friend,/ But rather means the spy—" (I, 179). He is not her friend; he is Altamont's. And, when he protests, "I come to prove myself Calista's friend," she will not believe him, especially when he continues to seek the cause of her discontentment. She refuses his friendship as she refuses the spiritual bonds of the marriage state; and, when Horatio suggests that guilt is the source of her sorrow, speaks out Lothario's name, and warns her never to see him again, she bursts out: "Dishonour blast thee, base, unmanner'd slave!/ That dar'st forget my birth, and sacred sex,/ And shock me with the rude unhallow'd sound" (I, 182). In reply, Horatio shows her the letter revealing her guilt.

Calista, furious at the sight of the letter, snatches it from Horatio's hands and tears it to pieces just as Altamont enters. Altamont's speech, beginning "Where is my Life, my Love, my charming Bride" (I, 182), turns to invective after Calista scornfully accuses him of being a party to the accusation. Because Altamont responds to Calista's wrath, he turns all his fury upon Horatio whose protest of friendship means nothing in the face of Altamont's wrath. Only the appearance of Lavinia at this moment stops their clash of swords. In the scene that follows, Rowe establishes another triangle: if the first puzzle is the relationship of Calista, Lothario, and Altamont, the second is that of Lavinia, Altamont, and Horatio. The first is the triangle of passionate love; the second, of conjugal bliss.

As Lavinia separates Altamont and Horatio, she attempts to find the cause of their quarrel; both of them are so overwrought that they are incoherent, and Altamont leaves without answering her plea, saying to Horatio, "From thy false friendship to her arms I'll fly" (I, 187). Horatio, broken-hearted about the perfidy of Calista and the loss of Altamont's friendship, is even more attentive to the situation in which Lavinia finds herself: she must choose, without proper knowledge, between her husband and her brother. Lavinia shared the loss of her father's wealth and reputation with Altamont; and, in her speech to Horatio, she remembers and prefigures a sad note that was later played for a brief turn in *Jane Shore*, Rowe's most celebrated examination of lost fortunes.

Altamont, appearing alone at the opening of Act IV, makes a kind
of summary of the play:

> With what unequal tempers are we form'd?
> One day the soul, supine with ease and fulness,
> Revels secure, and fondly tells herself,
> The hour of evil can return no more;
> The next, the spirits pall'd, and sick of riot,
> Turn all to discord, and we hate our beings.   (I, 188)

Calista, who has given him only "Coldness, aversion, tears, and
sullen sorrow," has left him to contemplate the loss of his friend
Horatio; Altamont's situation is difficult enough, but Calista's is
even more pathetic; for his account of their wedding night serves as
an emotional and psychological frame for the meeting of Lothario
and Calista. When Altamont leaves the stage, he just misses their
entrance into the garden for their ill-fated assignation that the letter
had arranged. To Lothario, their enjoyment of their love should be
continued:

> Weep not, my fair, but let the god of love
> Laugh in thy eyes, and revel in thy heart,
> Kindle again his torch, and hold it high,
> To light us to new joys; nor let a thought
> Of discord, or disquiet past, molest thee;
> But to a long oblivion give thy cares,
> And let us melt the present hour in bliss.   (I, 189)

When Calista replies, she rejects his advances and accuses him of
her ruin:

> Seek not to sooth me with thy false endearments,
> To charm me with thy softness: 'tis in vain;
> Thou canst no more betray, nor I be ruin'd.
> The hours of folly, and of fond delight,
> Are wasted all and fled:—
> . . . .
> I come to charge thee with a long account,
> Of all the sorrows I have known already,
> And all I have to come; thou hast undone me.   (I, 189)

But Lothario, with a touch of mockery, continues to support his view of their situation:

> Unjust *Calista!* dost thou call it ruin,
> To love as we have done; to melt, to languish,
> To wish for somewhat exquisitely happy,
> And then be blest ev'n to that wish's height?
> To die with joy, and strait to live again,
> Speechless to gaze, and with tumultuous transport.—   (I, 189)

Moreover, he will not agree that he has changed, has been false to her, or has been dishonorable; instead, he argues that she has been untrue to love, has fled from his arms, and has "wedded to another,/ Ev'n to the man whom most I hate on earth."(I, 190). His is the argument of passion, but in his speeches and in the poetry of this scene lie his sensual arguments. No lover can deny the validity of his argument, just as no honorable man could deny Altamont's wounded heart and honor.

While Lothario and Calista argue, Altamont appears at the back of the stage to hear Calista say "Hadst thou been true, how happy had I been?/ Not *Altamont*, but thou hadst been my lord" (I, 190). The complaints of love quite swiftly become the drama of revenge; for, a moment later, as Lothario and Altamont fight, Calista's cry of "Distraction! fury! sorrow! shame! and death!" indicates the tragic action of the play. Lothario is mortally wounded and dies; Calista snatches up his sword and offers to kill herself, but Altamont refuses to allow her to do so. The tragedy of her situation is not yet ended; its focus has simply been shifted from her own actions to those of the people who surround her—her new husband, her father, and their friends, Horatio and Lavinia. The shift from our involvement with Calista's plight to an examination of the motives and emotions of her associates requires a corresponding readjustment of our response to her. The unity of the play is not so much destroyed as it is refocused; and the last two acts succeed only to the degree that we are willing to participate in the complications of the debate between honor and love.

Wherever our own loyalties may lie, however, each character enacts his proper part on the stage. Sciolto would kill Calista, but Altamont prevents it. Calista, still determined in her course, would have her father end her wretched life so that she may escape her misery; there is nothing else left but that she "fly to some . . . dismal Place." Sciolto, still in a fury, would defy Altamont and give Calista her wish of just punishment; but he is not given the opportunity as, suddenly, the servants come in to report that Rossano has gathered a band of followers to avenge Lothario's death. Lavinia adds her account at this point by saying that she and Horatio were surrounded "by a mad multitude" and that she has left him defending himself against the mob. Altamont feels that he cannot endure the loss of his friend Horatio and would like to be reconciled to him. In the midst of Lavinia's report of violence, Horatio appears, breathless but unharmed.

Even with the clash of swords outside, Horatio, Lavinia, and Altamont debate their response to one another. Altamont's tragedy is deepened by the sharp contrast between the love and loyalty of his friends and the total refusal of Calista to give him any response other than cold scorn—even the response of pity. Testing the dimensions of friendship, Horatio finds he must forgive Altamont for his emotional outburst of anger as well as for his total involvement with Calista. As the act closes, Horatio and Lavinia pledge their support to Altamont; and Lavinia says, "We'll sit all day, and tell sad tales of love."

The last act of the play is quite brief, but it held a morbid fascination for the eighteenth-century audience. The use of spectacle and pageantry in Act V is adapted to the plot in such a way that it resolves the tangled action by answering the puzzle of the two dilemmas—the triangle of love and the triangle of friendship. The room is decorated in black; Lothario's body lies on a bier; a table bears skull and bones, a book, and a lamp; Calista, dressed in black, with her hair hanging loose, half reclines upon a couch. A macabre song of midnight, phantoms, and the tomb creates atmosphere for Calista's soliloquy that once again denies her personal tragedy. She contemplates the topic of death in both book and emblem, but the presence of the body of Lothario is much more real than any ghosts of the past or any doom of the future.

When her father enters to chide her again and to bewail his own position, Calista's attention remains upon her own sorrow rather than upon the tragedy she has brought upon her father. She has, she says, turned her eyes "inward upon myself." Death is the only refuge for her; she begs Sciolto to stab her. Sciolto cannot; because he is her father, he refuses to be her judge. Calista must add his grief to hers as she realizes for the first time that her misdeeds are not her concern alone but that they bring tragedy to family and friends as well as to herself.

When Sciolto leaves and Altamont enters, he reminds us of another dimension of the tragedy. Calista would wish for him some better fate than death—wish him "to live and be happy long;/ Live for some maid that shall deserve thy goodness." But this happiness can never be; for, having suffered the tragedy of their abortive relationship, Altamont can never achieve simple happiness and goodness. Their conversation is broken into abruptly by Horatio who brings the news that Sciolto has been wounded by Lothario's faction and is dying. Since this news is more than Calista can bear, she considers herself "contagion, death, and ruin" and stabs herself before Horatio and Altamont can stop her. When Sciolto, who is brought in as she is dying, offers her forgiveness, she asks for the mercy of heaven. Altamont, as he realizes her death, voices his response, and ours as well, when he declares:

> . . . Hadst thou a thousand faults,
> What heart so hard, what virtue so severe
> But at that beauty must of force relented,
> Melted to pity, love, and to forgiveness?   (I, 207)

Sciolto dies blessing Altamont who, overcome with grief, faints and is borne away. Horatio, who makes the last speech of the play, indicates that "By such examples are we taught to prove/ The sorrows that attend unlawful love."

In the Prologue, spoken by Betterton, who played the role of Horatio at the first performance, Rowe states that his play will present "A melancholy tale of private woes:/ No Princes here lost Royalty bemoan,/ But you shall meet with sorrows like your own" (I, 156). By the end of this declaration in which Calista's position is already clearly marked before her appearance on the stage, she had, no doubt, the sympathetic attention of that important segment of the audience that might be, or could become, the "yielding fair." Rowe's plays had already found approval before his presentation of *The Fair Penitent*, but with this "Tale of private woes" each fair one in the audience could identify as she pleased. As Rowe is made to say in *A New Rehearsal*, "I have not only the Favour of the Men of Quality, but of the Ladies too";[6] in 1703, moreover, *The Fair Peni-*

tent was "an ultra-modern play, whose heroine . . . spoke and acted in a manner similar to that of other young females of the day."[7]

The anticipation of the tragic consequences of Calista's act extends, in fact, far beyond its involvement in the action of the plot of *The Fair Penitent;* it engages the spectators in a kind of puzzle to resolve the moral issues as well as the physical ones. The eighteenth century had already become interested in debating such dilemmas. In John Dunton's popular publication, *The Athenian Mercury,* the puzzles of love and the proper solutions to them had held its audience for several issues of the weekly journal.[8]

Rowe does not stop the action to debate the ambiguities of Calista's position as he did with the theme of ambition in *Tamerlane;* he does not have to—his audience will do it for him. No matter how lightly such a situation might have been treated in Restoration comedy, it could not be treated lightly in 1703. The virtuous Queen Mary, still remembered with prayers, had been succeeded by the pious Queen Anne. As the events of Act I become increasingly sharp, so does our realization of our involvement in the play. Is it indeed not possible to be "The maid, the wife, the mistress, and the friend?" How are we to regard Calista? Do we support her entirely because she gave all to love? How are we to feel about Altamont's position? Is he to be pitied or must we see the situation as one Sciolto has created by arranging the match for his own purpose? And what must be Horatio's role as Altamont's friend and as the recipient of Sciolto's generosity? The answers to these questions affect both the succeeding action of the play and our response to it. The questions themselves help to explain the popularity of the play in the eighteenth century.[9]

II *The Responses to the Play*

From the original presentation throughout the century, *The Fair Penitent* was one of the most frequently performed of contemporary tragedies. Like Dante's Francesca and Goethe's Margarete, Calista herself—her character, her problems, her sorrows—has served as a focus of critical discussion of the universal and timeless conflict between love and honor and between the individual's response to his own heart and his obligation to society.[10] Many of Calista's critics have condemned her because she is never penitent, only sorry. As Johnson observes in his *Life of Rowe,* " . . . the title of the play does not sufficiently correspond with the behaviour of Calista, who at last

shews no evident signs of repentance, but may be reasonably sus-
pected of feeling pain from detection rather than guilt, and ex-
presses more shame than sorrow, more rage than shame." Johnson
thought, however, that the play was "one of the most pleasing
tragedies on the stage."[11]

In the "Prologue Sent to Mr. Rowe . . . but refus'd," an anonymous
writer inveighed against Rowe and his heroine:

> He from the Sock the PROSTITUTE transplants,
> And swells the *humble Whore* with Buskin Rants.
> His whore, indeed, repents the slippery Fault,
> But, like the rest, it is not 'til she's caught.
> She is not sorry, that she has Plaid the whore,
> But that, discover'd she can do't no more.[12]

As one twentieth-century critic also points out, "there is lamenta-
tion on Calista's part and a grim acceptance of death for her fault as
inevitable and just, but no accent of genuine contrition."[13]

Mrs. Inchbald in her "Remarks" that preface her edition of the
play also agrees that, "though [Calista] laments her fall from virtue
with all the anguish of degraded pride, she is still enamoured of the
cause from whence her guilt originated, and feels deeper sorrow
from her lover's abated passion (the natural consequence of her
frailty) than from motives of contrition." Mrs. Inchbald felt, however, that in her own time, "since the ladies of Great Britain have
learnt to spell, and have made other short steps in the path of
literature, the once highly favored Lothario of illiterate times has
sunk in estimation, and there is scarcely a woman in this country
who can sympathize in the grief of the fair penitent. . . ."[14]

Late in the eighteenth century in the revised edition of the *Biographia Dramatica*, Baker ends his review with the observation that
"this play is so well known, and is so frequently performed, and
always with the greatest applause, that little need be said of it.
. . ."[15] For *The Fair Penitent* to have remained so popular a play for so
long a time supports the original intention of Rowe himself when he
chose "an humbler theme" for his "she-tragedy" than those of his
Ambitious Step-Mother and *Tamerlane*.[16] Moreover, *The Fair Penitent* is the first and in some ways the most representative of Rowe's
"she-tragedies" because he has not yet developed either the sentimentalism he later exploits in *Lady Jane Gray* or the degeneration
of Jane in *Jane Shore*.

CHAPTER 5

The Biter: *A Comedy of Manners*

A FTER *The Fair Penitent*, Rowe's next play was a comedy, *The Biter*, which was first performed at Lincoln's Inn Fields in 1704 and which was published by Jacob Tonson in 1705. Most of the contemporary critics declared it to be unsuccessful; as a result, this work has been dismissed as being too slight and unimportant to examine. Almost invariably only two things have been said about it—the first is an anecdote from Pope (subsequently recorded by Spence) in which he said of Rowe, "Why he would laugh all day long! He would do nothing else but laugh!"; the second is Johnson's dismissal of the play: "finding that he [Rowe] and the public had no sympathy of mirth, he tried at lighter scenes no more."[1] The play, however, is not so poor as such comments might suggest; in fact, it is clever throughout and at times witty; but it is far from the kind of comedy of manners that many of the audience doubtless remembered.

Actually, such comedy was not being written in 1704, for William Congreve had finished his career in 1700 with *The Way of the World*. Although he had done his part to support his position and that of his colleagues in the controversy that had occurred after the publication of Jeremy Collier's *A Short View of the Immorality and Profaneness of the English Stage* in 1698, Congreve never again wrote an example to illustrate his contention that "the Vices most frequent, and which are the common Practice of the looser sort of Livers, are the subject Matter of Comedy."[2]

Whatever play Congreve might have written would perhaps not have pleased the public taste any better than Rowe's comedy did, for the old comedy of wit was rapidly being replaced with one that focused on plot and situation—the kind of play that appealed to the interests of a middle-class, not an aristocratic, audience. *The Biter* may serve as an example of this new kind of play that gave no offense to any member of the audience whether it succeeded dramatically or not. As a matter of fact, it ran for six performances in 1704 and was revived in 1716 and again in 1746. To conclude that Rowe and his public "had no sympathy for mirth" is quite inaccurate.

I *The Farce of* The Biter

The situation of *The Biter* is a simple one—Sir Timothy Tallapoy, an elderly father, now a rich merchant, has a beautiful but independent daughter Angelica for whom he would choose a suitable husband. Sir Timothy consults neither his daughter nor the bridegroom designate; indeed, he has never seen the young man. All is arranged by the two fathers, who themselves do not know each other. The young man's father is a country squire; and Sir Timothy, determined Angelica will not marry one of the London beaux, arranges the match simply by his own authority. In almost all such cases of arranged marriages the choices are wrong and, in addition, are frequently ludicrous; and Sir Timothy's choice is both. Pinch, the young man he selects, is a fool and a knave; he is, as he himself says, a biter, and when he comes upon the scene, both his appearance and his actions define the word. Insolent and stupid, he pretends to be a wit and a man-about-town; he is neither.

In an early *Tatler* paper, Steele has a dialogue in White's Chocolate House between Mr. Friendly, "a reasonable Man of the Town," and Acorn, "an honest Englishman of good plain sense and meaning" during the course of which Friendly defines a biter as "a dull fellow that tells you a lye with a grave face and laughs at you for knowing him no better than to believe him."[3] Both Steele's definition of the word "biter" and his character, Mr. Friendly, "a reasonable Man of the Town," suggest Rowe's play. Rowe's Pinch is certainly "a dull fellow," and his Friendly is the name of the young man Angelica has chosen for herself.

The plot of the play is simple and direct. Since Sir Timothy has never seen Pinch, he is easy to deceive. Angelica and Friendly contrive for Sir Timothy to see Pinch under such adverse circumstances that, when Pinch somewhat later meets Sir Timothy again to present himself as the young squire designed to be Angelica's bridegroom, Sir Timothy will refuse to believe that Pinch can possibly be the young man he himself has chosen. Clerimont, Sir Timothy's nephew, and Mariana, Friendly's kinswoman, who are secretly married to each other, are Angelica and Friendly's chief allies. However, Mrs. Clever, Scribblescrabble and his wife, along with an assortment of servants, also lend their somewhat disorganized aid.

The scene of the play is a country town during fair time; and the opening episodes take place before Sir Timothy's new house among the bustle and confusion of the crowds of country people. Sir Timothy has made his fortune in the East India trade, and no one dares mention "west" in his presence. With his fortune, he has acquired a taste for things Chinese. He has named his new house *Kingquangcungxi;* for, as Maria explains, "You must know he got his Estate by the *China* Trade in the *East-Indies,* and at that time grew so fond of the Manners, Language, Habit, and everything that relates to those People. . . . 'Tis ridiculous enough to see how he makes himself be dress'd and serv'd exactly after the *Chinese* manner" (I, 223). The house is filled with Chinese objects; he fancies that he uses Chinese manners; and, after he arranges for Angelica's marriage, he is resolved to marry Mariana "and engender a Male Off-spring, who shall drink nothing but the Divine Liquor Tea, and eat nothing but Oriental Rice, and be brought up after the Institutions of the most excellent *Confucius*" (I, 230).

Immediately before Sir Timothy sees Pinch and Scribblescrabble for the first time, he has had a quarrel with a servant who has broken his "great Pagode"; and, since he has already had a sharp and unpleasant argument with Angelica, he is in no mood to be reasonable. As he comes upon the stage and encounters Pinch, who has just arrived by stage coach from London, Sir Timothy asks about news from London. When Pinch replies, "There's Comical News, Faith, in the *Flying-Post*—It's given out and rumour'd, that several Great Men, and *Beglerbegs* in the *West-Indies,* have declar'd for the Rebels in Hungary" (I, 231), Sir Timothy makes an angry speech about all things that have to do with "west," will not listen to any explanation of what Pinch meant, and begins to beat him soundly with his stick until Clerimont, coming upon the stage, interposes. After such an incident, the outcome of Angelica's plan to refuse her father's choice of a husband is never in doubt. Given the encounter between Pinch and Sir Timothy and the insurance provided by the fact that Mariana "engag'd a notable limb of the law, a city solicitor" to outwit Sir Timothy, Angelica can hardly be in much danger. In fact, the farce of Sir Timothy's first meeting with Pinch ensures a happy ending for Angelica. The rest of the play works out her scheme.

II *The Characters and Devices of the Play*

The characters of the play are stock characters quite as much as the situation of the plot is conventional. There is the "affected amorous old widow," Lady Stale, who is in pursuit of Friendly and to whom Friendly must be polite no matter how much he may wish to concentrate on working out his plan to marry Angelica. Mrs. Clever, Lady Stale's friend, is the gossip who is used in this play as an aid for the young lovers rather than as the hindrance such characters sometimes are devised to be. Her character is among the more interesting variations Rowe has created since she is used to manipulate the other characters and is largely responsible for the episodes that comprise the entertainment of the play. In her conversation, she serves as a foil to Lady Stale; she reveals Lady Stale's extremely foolish foibles and affectations. She has known Scribblescrabble and his wife in the past, and she prepares the group to laugh at the wife's drunken antics when Scribblescrabble and his wife appear. A partner in wit with Mariana, Mrs. Clever represents, in fact, the most sophisticated point of view in the play, for she maintains throughout it that "Matrimony's an uncertain Game."

The character of Pinch is an undistinguished one in every way. Indeed, his only real distinction is that he is so determinedly undistinguished. Not really clever even in his attempt to assume the role of a fop, he overplays and overemphasizes the emptiness of his type in such a way that his example serves in part to work out the situation of the play and in part to make the comment that, as Steele's Friendly says, he is "an impudent creature made up of vice only, who supports his ignorance by his courage and want of learning by contempt of it."[4]

Angelica and Mariana are two attractive young women who, despite their feminine wiles, make their own conclusion to their plans by using both ingenuity and discretion. Mariana is already married secretly to Clerimont, Sir Timothy's nephew, before the opening of the play; and the fact that she deliberately manipulates Sir Timothy to her own purpose when he has designed her for his own wife adds a nice, piquant touch to his defeat. Angelica's pertness and her clever execution of the plan to make Sir Timothy himself dismiss Pinch make her role in the play a pleasant diversion. In Rowe's tragedies, two such beautiful heroines would have spoken and behaved in a far different manner.

The secret marriage, already a favorite device for Rowe, is used effectively in *The Biter;* but he had already used this long-standing convention of Restoration and eighteenth-century drama in *The Ambitious Step-Mother* and in *Tamerlane.* In none of these plays, however, is the marriage ever consummated; and each time the bride comes to a tragic end—Amestris is stabbed; Arpasia dies of a broken heart after she sees her husband strangled. In *The Biter,* Mariana's situation is never a dangerous one although Sir Timothy is quite outspoken about his intention to marry her. It hardly seems possible that Fate would dare to intervene in the plans of either Mariana or Angelica, and Sir Timothy is certainly not cast in the dimensions of any kind of supernatural being. In fact, the very idea that he could in any way impose his will either as a father on Angelica or as a husband on Mariana is the basic farcical situation of the play. Both Angelica and Mariana are the kind of clever, strong-minded women who make men like Sir Timothy seem merely eccentric and petulant. Doubtless Rowe's audience recognized him; there were Sir Timothys on every hand, and his portrayal as a successful merchant in the China trade added a bit of extra color to a familiar domestic situation.

III   *The Judgment of the Play*

It would certainly be futile to argue that Rowe's comedy was anything more than a pleasant evening's entertainment, but it must have served as a diverting comment on the rising interest in things Oriental and as a gentle criticism of the current interest in "biting." Like all the other comedies of its kind, it made comments about the eternal battle of the sexes. Betterton played the part of Sir Timothy in the original production; and Lowe, Betterton's biographer, defends both Rowe and the play in his account when he says: "It is a brisk bustling farce, with an amusing plot, good humorous characters, and fairly bright dialogue. Johnson tells the story of Rowe's sitting in the theatre laughing vehemently at his own jokes while no one else smiled; but the anecdote lacks confirmation, for the piece ran six nights, and it is difficult to imagine that any audience should have been so depressed by a farce as to sit so mumchance as the story implies."[5] One twentieth-century critic has called it "worse than dull,"[6] but for the eighteenth century it remained a stock play; for as we have already indicated, it appeared at intervals throughout the century.

CHAPTER 6

Ulysses *and* The Royal Convert:
Plays of Patriotism

WHATEVER Rowe's own estimate of the success or failure of his comedy *The Biter* may have been, he turned again to tragedy in *Ulysses* and in *The Royal Convert*, his next two plays. *Ulysses* was presented November 22, 1705, in the Haymarket; it ran until December 1. Two years later, *The Royal Convert* was produced on November 25, 1707, and ran for six nights. Twentieth-century critics consider neither of these plays to have been significant. To Baker, *Ulysses* "was acted . . . with success; but is not the best of this author's pieces." He found *The Royal Convert* more to his taste.[1]

In a discussion of Rowe's work, however, these plays are of great importance. They reflect the topics and tastes of their own contemporary world more directly than do his three earlier plays; and, as in the earlier plays, they show Rowe creating the soft, passionate lovers who later become the basis for his "she-tragedies." For an understanding of Rowe, these tragedies cannot be neglected.

I *Rowe's Personal Life, 1703–1707*

In Rowe's own personal life the years after 1703, when *The Fair Penitent* was produced, to 1707, when *The Royal Convert* was presented, were rather uncertain ones. There is no evidence to show that Rowe continued to practice law after his early success in the theater, but he must have remained active as a Whig. In 1705, he wrote to George Savile, Marquis of Halifax, asking for a place in his employ; but he was unsuccessful. Another incident of these years is the story recounted in a conversation between Spence and Pope. Pope, speaking of Halifax, said, "It was he who advised Mr. Rowe to learn Spanish, and after all his pains and expectation, only said, 'Then, Sir, I envy you the pleasure of reading *Don Quixote* in the original."[2]

Whether the story is true or not, it indicates that Rowe, like most of his friends, was interested in the patronage of government as well as in success as a writer; but he also was motivated by personal problems. Rowe's wife died in 1706, and their infant daughter had been buried at St. Paul's on August 16, 1705. After his wife's death, Rowe sold at least a part of his estate in Devonshire "for the uses of his marriage settlement, and the residue for the payment of debts."[3] In view of such personal problems, it is perhaps not surprising that Rowe wrote to please what he thought to be the received opinion and taste of his contemporaries. This intention becomes obvious from a close reading of *Ulysses* and *The Royal Convert*. The ways in which he achieved this representative quality make the plays significant, then, not only in themselves but also for Rowe's theater and his personal life.

II *The Material of* Ulysses

Ulysses is based on the familiar account of the hero's return and his triumph over Penelope's arrogant and wasteful suitors. Except for the background and broad outlines of the plot, however, the incidents of Rowe's play are his own. Two lines of dramatic action run parallel through most of the play: that of Ulysses and his return to Penelope and that of Telemachus and his love for Semanthe. The two stories touch only at two tragic moments: first, where Telemachus, defending his mother, kills Semanthe's father, Eurymachus; and, second, when Semanthe, who decides her love for Telemachus is greater than her need for true revenge, falsely accuses Antinous of the murder.

Within the two stories about the return of Ulysses and about Telemachus' love for Semanthe, Rowe again repeats familiar themes. Again we have the secret, unconsummated marriage—a situation used in *Tamerlane*, which is now the plight of Telemachus and Semanthe—and the picture of ideal wedded love between Ulysses and Penelope, one even more ideal in quality than that of Horatio and Lavinia in *The Fair Penitent*. In addition, we find the familiar themes of ambition, rebellion, pride, and greed among those who would fill Ulysses' long-vacant throne. The variations are more conventional in their development, however, than they were in Rowe's earlier plays. The loyalty of Penelope to Ulysses is the traditional one of Homer's poem, and the willingness of Telemachus and Semanthe to sacrifice their happiness in response to filial obligations helps to work out the traditional responses to the family loyalties suggested in the original poem. Moreover, Rowe returns through these themes to the heroic drama of his earlier plays and to those of his predecessors Otway and Lee.

III   *The Action of* Ulysses

Rowe opens *Ulysses* with a conversation between Telemachus and Mentor as they review the long years since the conclusion of the Trojan war and recall how "Riot, wrong, and woeful desolation,/ Spread o'er the wretched land, . . ." (II, 8). Their conversation is very soon interrupted, however, by Aethon, who appears as Ulysses' old friend but who is actually Ulysses himself in disguise. Antinous, coming upon the scene, reports to Telemachus a favorable message from Semanthe, described as "the fair/ The gentle, the forgiving . . ." (II, 9). When Antinous and Telemachus leave to seek her, Mentor and Aethon remain to discuss the state of Ithaca and the sad circumstances of Penelope. Aethon, having noticed the rapport between Antinous and Telemachus, questions Mentor about the relationship between Antinous and the queen. Mentor replies that Penelope has repulsed Antinous and "Taught him to bend his abject head to earth/ And own his humbler lot . . ." (II, 9).

Before Ulysses (Aethon) can conclude his estimation of Antinous, a group of angry suitors arrives. They have discovered Penelope's deceit, the riddle of her mystic web; and, when Ulysses reprimands them for their noise and rioting, they turn upon him to silence his reproof. After Ulysses defends his right to freedom of opinion and speech, Eurymachus, the king of Samos and Semanthe's father, steps forth as a leader among the suitors. And with the appearance of Penelope herself upon the scene the principal actors in the conflict have been introduced. A series of set speeches follows in which each suitor offers in turn his praise of the queen and his rights to be considered her husband. There is in the exchange a courtly pageant of the virtues and powers of a queen, which are summarized by Ulysses when he alone remains on stage; plot and themes have all been introduced by the end of this scene.

The rivalry among the suitors is nicely complicated. Eurymachus is not alone in having plans to possess the queen. Antinous, the chief of the lords of Ithaca, is urged by his fellow countrymen to wed their queen himself, rid them of Eurymachus, and save them from a foreign yoke. Encouraged by their words, Antinous reveals that, to

confound both Eurymachus and Penelope, he has fostered Telemachus' love for Eurymachus' daughter, Semanthe, even to the
point of helping them wed secretly. As Antinous and his friends
leave, the two lovers appear. They have just come from the marriage ceremony, but Semanthe is already full of foreboding instead
of joy. Before she had come to Ithaca, she had vowed to belong to
Artemis, the virgin goddess—vows she has now broken. Telemachus comforts her in vain, and their melancholy scene is followed
by an even more serious one when the queen is confronted by
Eurymachus, whose insistence is seconded this time by Ulysses,
who is still disguised as Aethon. From soft and tender words at first,
Eurymachus turns to angry threats to destroy Telemachus if he
cannot win Penelope. She, in turn, rejects both his tenderness and
his angry threats; but she eventually realizes that he will indeed
carry out his threat if she refuses his offer of marriage. Thoroughly
frightened, she consents to allow him to come to her chambers at
sunset, hoping in this way to gain the time to make some plan of
escape.

Throughout the scene Penelope is the ideal wife and mother as
she tries desperately to deny Eurymachus without endangering her
son. Ulysses' presence in the scene makes more real her tragic
despair as she sees no escape from Eurymachus' wickedness. Still
unrevealed, Ulysses is sent away to conduct the priest who will
perform the forced marriage; and the scene and the act end with his
vow to bring full and speedy revenge upon Eurymachus and his
kind. The first scene of Act III develops the sorrow of the queen as,
thinking she is alone, she reviews her situation. Ulysses, Mentor,
and Eumaeus hear her and come forward to speak when she suddenly offers to stab herself, only to be stopped by Ulysses.
Penelope, thinking him allied with Eurymachus, had banished him
from her sight; but, turning to him now, she cries, "Off! Off, thou
traitor" (II, 37). Admonishing Mentor and Eumaeus to calm her,
Ulysses leaves as the queen turns to them to voice her sorrow:

> And are you too my foes? have you conspir'd
> And join'd with that false *Aethon* to betray me?
> Here sit thee down then, humbly in the dust,
> Here sit, a poor forlorn, abandon'd woman:
> Cast not thy eyes up to yon azure firmament,
> Nor hope relief from thence, the Gods are pitiless,
> Or busy in their heav'n and thou not worth their care. . . .   (II, 37)

But the gods are not pitiless: suddenly, when Mentor and Eumaeus add their prayers to hers, the heavens unfold to reveal Pallas Athena in all her glory. Eumaeus, Mentor, and Penelope kneel in her presence; and, before the magic of the scene is gone, Penelope turns to see Aethon appear and become Ulysses as he drops his disguise and appears in his own form. Their happy reunion is followed immediately by another when Telemachus joins them, and his father asks his aid in revenging his wrongs at the hands of the suitors. In solemn ceremony Telemachus pledges to guard his mother and to deny anyone entrance to her chambers; but he does not know the double meaning of his vow. Ulysses knows, as Telemachus does not, that Eurymachus will be his antagonist; what Ulysses does not know is that Antinous has his own plot to win the prize, the queen.

Act IV begins with a scene between Antinous and Telemachus in which Telemachus tells of his father's return. In amazement, Antinous agrees to help defend both Penelope and Ulysses; secretly, however, he means to pursue his own plan to take Penelope for himself. Meanwhile, Eurymachus, arriving at the queen's quarters, finds Telemachus guarding them. Surely, Telemachus thinks, the gods will not exact revenge upon Eurymachus, Semanthe's father. Pleading with him politely, Telemachus refuses him entrance. Eurymachus will not be refused; in their brief fight, Eurymachus falls mortally wounded. Telemachus has chosen between his duty and his love; love has lost.

The scene that follows is one of the most dramatic in the play. Semanthe, lamenting the sorrows of the queen, finds her father slain by her husband's hand. In one breath she calls for justice from the gods for her father's murderer and utters the name of her dear husband, Telemachus. In his dying words, Eurymachus accuses Telemachus; but Semanthe cannot comprehend a truth she cannot face. Telemachus, returning, kisses her back to consciousness only to hear her curse all false men. In his turn, he too is overcome and leaves his post; when Antinous appears, he cannot believe his good fortune—Eurymachus slain and Telemachus gone. He immediately orders his soldiers to "Come on, and let the crafty-fam'd Ulysses/ Repine and rage, . . . Let the forsaken husband vainly mourn" (II, 56).

Between the fourth and fifth acts, Antinous's evil purpose is accomplished; he gains entrance to the queen. All seems to be lost—Eumaeus, Mentor, and Ulysses are caught between the perfidy of

Antinous and the Samians, who "call loud for vengeance" upon the slayer of their ruler. Semanthe's love provides deliverance, for she accuses Antinous of her father's murder and her retainers drive Antinous and his followers away to revenge the death of Eurymachus. In the final scene, Ulysses and Penelope are united; Telemachus, forgiven; Semanthe, returned to her homeland and her vows. Ulysses ends the play with proper reverence to the gods while giving comfort to his son, because of the loss of his beloved.

IV *The Theme of Wedded Love in* Ulysses

When Johnson wrote about Rowe's *Ulysses*, his estimate was that "We have been too early acquainted with the poetical heroes to expect any pleasure from their revival; to shew them as they have already been shewn, is to disgust by repetition; to give them new qualities or new adventures, is to offend by violating received notions."[4] Contrary to Johnson's views, however, Rowe's variations are both interesting and significant; and the play certainly does not "offend by violating received notions." As we have indicated, the twin themes of the play are expressed by the ideal wedded love between Ulysses and Penelope and by the tragedy of secret love between Telemachus and Semanthe; within each of these two themes are many variations.

Penelope is the ideal wife, faithful, loyal, and careful—careful beyond her personal relationship to her husband, for she has maintained Ulysses' kingdom for him during his absence. Rowe's Prologue immediately places Penelope as the most important person in the play and suggests at the same time a contemporary tone. Penelope was

> a virtuous wife:
> A lady, who, for twenty years, withstood
> The pressing instances of flesh and blood;
> Her husband, still a man of sense reputed,
> . . . .
> Left her at ripe eighteen, to seek renown,
> . . . .
> To fill his place, fresh lovers came in shoals,
> . . . .
> They sent her billets-doux, and presents many,
> Of ancient tea and Thericlean china;
> Rail'd at the Gods, toasted her o'er and o'er,

> Dress'd at her, danc'd, and fought, and sigh'd, and swore;
> ....
> But all in vain, the virtuous dame stood buff,
> And let 'em know that she was coxcomb proof. . . . (II, 5)

Like Penelope, Rowe says, English wives can be true too:

> We have our chaste Penelopes, who mourn
> Their widow'd beds, and wait their Lords return,
> We have our heroes too, who bravely bear,
> Far from their home, the dangers of the war;
> Who careless of the winter season's rage,
> New toils explore, and in new cares engage;
> From realm to realm their chief unweary'd goes,
> And restless journies on, to give the world repose. (II, 5)

Moreover, the English queen was herself an example for all to emulate.

V   *Penelope and Queen Anne*

In 1705, when *Ulysses* was produced, the War of the Spanish Succession had settled into a somewhat familiar pattern of being always a part of English foreign policy; at home, "the principle of 'Peace at home and war abroad' was triumphant."[5] In the fall of the year, Parliament was especially concerned again with the succession. The problem of maintaining favor with Queen Anne while at the same time making a successful guess as to how to cultivate favor with a future (at present very uncertain) monarch was a constantly recurring one throughout Anne's reign. An invalid when she became queen, Anne was not expected to live very long; she was much beloved by her subjects; and everyone, from high to low, knew that she very much opposed the idea of setting up a rival court for her "successor" while she remained in command of her faculties and the throne.[6]

In October, 1705, when the new Parliament convened, the queen urged the necessity of the union with Scotland, encouraged support of the war with optimistic reports about its progress, and reaffirmed vigorously her support for the Church of England. In reply to the Earl of Rochester, the queen's uncle, and his group, a majority in Parliament voted "that 'whoever goes about to suggest and insinuate that the Church is in danger under Her Majesty's administration, is an enemy to the Queen, the Church and the Kingdom.' "[7] Convocation, the official assembly of the Church of England, was meeting at the same time as Parliament; and among the things the clergy complained of was the immorality of the theater. Also during the winter there was, as had become usual, much debate and discussion about the war and the Allies. And against all these current disagreements and factions, there was the shifting treachery of the Jacobites and the near Jacobites who, seeing themselves out of favor with Anne, provided for their future "place" by settling firmly the Hanoverian succession.[8]

It was moved in the House of Lords to invite Sophia, the Dowager Electress of Hanover, to come to England to live and thus be present to insure the succession. But Queen Anne's friends, knowing how she felt, were resourceful enough to defeat the bill and to pass instead the Regency Act which provided the means whereby the Protestant Succession would occur after the death of the queen, but the Hanoverians would not come to England until they came to the throne. In the end, Sophia died before Queen Anne; but the Regency Act placed George I in power when Anne died and left almost no way for the Pretender to create rebellion at that crucial moment.

All these decisions and triumphs did not occur without much discussion and debate, for the speeches continued throughout the fall. The Tory lords, arguing that Anne was ill and that she might become "as a child in the hands of others," alienated Anne more and more as she listened with consternation to their proposals, especially as she had been led to believe by this same group of Tory lords that "to invite over the Successor in her lifetime, had [been] designed to depose her."[9] The Regency Act was drawn up and presented to Parliament in the closing weeks of the year.

Precisely at this time, during the debate about the Regency Act, Rowe's *Ulysses* was performed and published. There is little doubt that the audience would have failed to realized Rowe's point of view. Clearly Penelope, the queen, dominated his play just as their Queen Anne had dominated Parliament. Moreover, as the prize to be captured by foreign suitors and by dissident subjects, Penelope, in her experience, showed forth the struggle to control Anne. Rochester and the Tory lords, like Antinous in the play, would have her in their control if they could devise a way to do so. Moreover, all these points which were made clear in the play as it was performed were doubly underscored in the published version.

The structure of the plot that revolves about Penelope may offer an interesting puzzle. Most of the episodes are suggested from the traditional situation of Penelope and her suitors, but Antinous, the principal contender for her hand among the Ithacans, is said to be

> Noble by birth, and mighty in his wealth,
> Proud of the patriot's name and peoples praise,
> By gifts, by friendly offices and eloquence,
> He won the herd of Ithacans to think him
> E'en worthy to supply his master's place.   (II, 10)

Moreover, his rejection by the queen is caused by his presumptuous ambition as reported by Mentor, who says that Penelope

> Taught him to bend his abject head to earth,
> And own his humbler lot—He stood rebuk'd
> And full of guilty sorrow for the past,
> Vow'd to repeat the daring crime no more,
> But with humility and loyal service
> To purge his fame, and wash the stains away.   (II, 10–11)

But Ulysses in his disguise as Aethon will not accept the change that Mentor describes; instead, he thinks

>   . . . the turns too sudden;
> Habitual evils seldom change so soon,
> But many days must pass, and many sorrows,
> Conscious remorse and anguish must be felt,
> To curb desire, to break the stubborn will,
> And work a second nature in the soul,
> Ere virtue can resume the place she lost;
> 'Tis else dissimulation—   (II, 11)

Whatever Antinous's part may have been in the plot of the play, his description here suggests he may be very like the Earl of Rochester, the queen's uncle, or, if not Rochester, then perhaps the Duke of Marlborough. Both, accustomed to great power, had in the months of 1705–1706 lost favor with the queen.[10]

When the suitors appear to compliment the queen in the manner of Restoration courtiers, Ulysses, looking at them, says, "'Tis well the Gods are mild, when these dare hope/ To merit their best gifts by riot and injustice." And, when Ulysses, still disguised, quarrels with Ephialtes, the queen rejects both contention and flattery; she will consider no one except "that brave man/ That dares avenge me well upon the rest" (II, 16). Later, when Aethon (Ulysses) offers to aid Eurymachus, he argues that Penelope is first of all a woman, which means she is "wanton" and "must be try'd"; and he promises that she will be

> Thro' all the winding mazes of her thoughts,
> Thro' all her joys, her sorrows, and her fears,
> Thro' all her truth and falsehood I'll pursue her.
> She shall be subtler than deceit itself,
> And prosperously wicked if she 'scape me.   (II, 19)

Penelope's subsequent behavior belies such judgment, and the sharp contrast between their measure of her and her steadfast loyalty to her own principles dramatically reinforces the view that some of the fair sex may be tried and found true. In the episode in which Eurymachus presses his claims upon her, she begins to show her strength when she says to Aethon, "Answer, I charge thee, to this cruel King; Demand if it be noble to prophane/ My virtue thus, with loose dishonest courtship" (II, 30). When Aethon seems to desert her to side with Eurymachus, she accuses him of "dissembled friendship" and banishes him from her sight. Moments later, however, when Eurymachus makes it quite plain that he will force her by siezing Telemachus, she becomes desperate as she understands that she must choose between her virtue as the spotless wife and her devotion as the faultless mother. Her speech at this point makes clear her dilemma:

> Oh thou dear youth, for whom I feel again
> My throes, and twice endure a mother's pain;
> Well had I died to save thee, Oh my son,
> Well, to preserve thy life, had giv'n my own;
> But when the thoughts of former days return,
> When my lost virtue, fame, and peace I mourn
> The joys which still thou gav'st me I forget,
> And own I bought thee at a price too great.   (II, 32–33)

Within this context of loyal devotion to her husband and to her son, we see her greatness. Any choice she makes must be a tragic one. Unlike the cynical discussion Aethon and Eurymachus have of her "sex's weakness," Penelope's view is that of a "mother's fondness in my eyes and all her tender passions in my heart" (II, 36). In her desperation Penelope offers to kill herself; but she is saved, and almost immediately her salvation is revealed to be from the gods in the appearance of Pallas Athena and from her husband when Ulysses abandons his disguise.

Caught in the immediate drama of Penelope's story, the spectators no doubt followed the speeches of first one and then another as Aethon, Eurymachus, and Penelope argued her position; but a moment of reflection must have reminded them of their Queen Anne's personal tragedy. Deeply devoted to her father and her husband, she had, nevertheless, been crowned queen instead of offering the crown to her father's son; and she had suffered the tragic loss of one child after another with the final, especially pathetic, death of her only remaining child, the little Duke of Gloucester in 1700. After his death, she had listened to the debate over the Protestant Succession while William made firm the succession to her instead of to the Pretender James III as she, so important a factor in the scheme, sat silently by. Anne's choice of remaining loyal to her British subjects rather than to her father and his son when her own children have died, makes the dilemma debated by Penelope far more topical for Rowe's audience than for his later readers. Seemingly abandoned by everyone, but kept from death, Penelope says to Mentor:

> And are you too my foes? have you conspir'd
> And join'd with that false Aethon to betray me?
> Here sit thee down then, humbly in the dust,
> Here sit, a poor forlorn, abandon'd woman. . . .   (II, 37)

and, in the presence of Pallas Athena, she prays, "Virgin, begot and born of *Jove* alone,/ Chaste, wise, victorious . . . Once more be favourable—be propitious, . . ." (II, 38). Each speech could be lifted out of the context of the play and given to Anne herself. And, when Ulysses makes himself known, the Queen says "Nay 'tis, 'tis most impossible to reason,/ But what have I to do with thought or reason?" To which Ulysses replies:

> No, live thou great example of thy sex,
> Live for the world, for me, and for thyself,
> Unnumber'd blessings, honors, years of happiness,

> Crowns from the Gods, enrich'd with brightest stars,
> All heav'n and earth united in applause,
> Wait, with officious duty, to reward thee.   (II, 39)

Both speeches fit Queen Anne's own immediate situation in 1705.

Following the recognition scene, the whole action of the play is turned toward Queen Penelope, both as a physical and a psychological prize. Telemachus, left to defend her, creates his own tragedy by slaying Eurymachus, his wife's father. The price Telemachus pays, the death of Eurymachus, and the defeat of Antinous all seem to make the prize of Penelope and her safety of the greatest importance. It is she around whom the whole government turns; and, when she and Ulysses are finally united, the danger to the kingdom is over as well as the personal danger to themselves. If Parliament and the public needed to be reminded of the possible virtues of an ideal queen—their ideal queen—Rowe had reminded them in the role of Penelope.

VI   *The Theme of Young Love*

In the other major theme of the play, the story of Telemachus and Semanthe, Rowe shows the proper way for young lovers to behave. Since Telemachus is first of all the son of Penelope and Ulysses, his honor rests upon his defending his mother. His father's command makes no compromise possible. He cannot do so up to a point and then refuse to complete his assignment. In fact, the family relationships between mother and son, father and son, and their interloyalties underlie the whole plot structure of the play. Finally, Telemachus and Semanthe's secret marriage brings about the tragedy of the play at the end: without their sad story, no note of pathos would have remained; with it, the pathos is extended to the plight of man himself.

If the study of Penelope as a queen spoke to the situation in the British Parliament, the story of Telemachus and Semanthe spoke to the complaints of the clergy about the evils of the theater. Surely no pair of lovers could be more virtuous and chaste than Telemachus and Semanthe—no one questions their relationship for itself or seeks to part them for evil purpose. Like Romeo and Juliet, they are victims of their families' quarrel; and their story is the more pathetic because they, unlike Romeo and Juliet, must live to deny their own happiness in support of the family.

Their first scenes in the play are the essence of young love. The irony of the situation that develops when both Eurymachus and Antinous use them and thus help to bring death to themselves as well as grief to Telemachus and tragedy to Semanthe does not stain the purity of their love for each other. In his first speech about Semanthe, Telemachus asks Antinous to speak softly because "wisdom and age/ Reason perversely when they judge of love" (II, 9). At first the only seeming ill omen to their happiness is Semanthe's vow to Cynthia to join her train and forego love. Her fateful dream of foreboding is forgotten as Telemachus with loving tenderness reassures her. His voice, his speech itself, bring back the happy omens; and the "good Gods are gracious" until she is overcome "with excess of happiness . . . 'Tis pain and pleasure blended, both at once,/'Tis life and death, or something more than either" (II, 25).

But when Semanthe comes, thinking to fulfill their tryst, the gods have already decreed their tragedy; and the groan Semanthe hears is that of her father as he lies fatally wounded by her husband. It is her turn to make a choice between love and honor, between her love for Telemachus and the need to revenge her father's death; she repeats Penelope's dilemma in different terms; and, like Penelope, she must lose by whatever choice she makes. If Penelope is to be happy, Telemachus and Semanthe cannot be. Semanthe's sad and bitter speech to Telemachus at the end of the scene concludes her spoken part in the play; her words are addressed to the audience as much as to him:

> Detested by the name of love for ever!
> Henceforth let easy maids be warn'd by men,
> No more to trust your breasts that heave with sighing,
> Your moving accents, and your melting eyes;
> Whene'er you boast your truth then you mean deceiving;
> If yet there should some fond believer be,
> Let the false man betray the wretch like thee,
> Like thee, the lost, repenting fool disclaim,
> For crowns, ambition, and your idol, fame. . . .   (II, 54)

With Telemachus and Semanthe, Rowe has played again a familiar theme—a secret and fatal marriage unconsummated; a beautiful, virtuous heroine victimized by circumstances. The variations of this theme in *Ulysses*, however, are peculiarly attractive. There is no lust, no violence, only sad resignation to duty—resignation that is the tacit sign of filial piety and duty to the Queen. While Semanthe's story does not reach the magnitude of Juliet's, it is gentler, less dramatic, and far more pathetic. Moreover, she is more directly involved in the action of the play, for her falsely naming Antinous as her father's murderer changes the whole conclusion of the play. She becomes thereby a major actor, unlike Ophelia or Desdemona, whose stories, however tragic, are beyond their control, whatever choice they might have made.

VII   *The Design and Plot of* The Royal Convert

Rowe's next play, *The Royal Convert*, was, like *Ulysses*, produced at the Haymarket by Betterton and his company; and, also like *Ulysses*, it was a serious poetic-patriotic commentary on the contemporary scene—this time with a quasi-historical background of British history rather than with the distant setting of Ithaca. Moreover, in this case there was no fable by Homer, so there could be no early acquaintance with the heroes "to disgust by repetition" or "to offend by violating received notions," as Johnson had suggested about *Ulysses*. In fact, Johnson, comparing *Ulysses* and *The Royal Convert*, says: "*The Royal Convert* seems to have a better claim to longevity. The fable is drawn from an obscure and barbarous age to which fictions are most easily and properly adapted; for when objects are imperfectly seen, they easily take forms from imagination."[11] *The Royal Convert* did indeed prove to be a more popular play than *Ulysses*.

In the Prologue, Rowe anticipates the criticism of his tragedy as "such damn'd grave stuff," and he hopes to place his play by appealing to more "equal judges." And the Epilogue, far lighter and less serious than the Prologue, repeats the idea that the play has a serious message, even though Rowe says, "To some I know, it may appear but odly:/ That this place of all others, should turn godly." There could hardly be a more direct appeal to the authorities and the clergy or a clearer indication of the patriotic-moral bias Rowe designed.

The play is set in Kent in the early years after the first invasion of Britain by the Saxons. The plot situation is in itself a classic one in that two brothers are in love with the same beautiful girl. In the case of *The Royal Convert*, however, Rowe has been unusually skillful in his dramaturgy; from the rivalry of the two brothers he has made a complex series of incidents sustain a serious examination of the relationships between state and church; and, perhaps even more skillfully, the personal relationships of a king are examined in his role as ruler and statesman as related to his private, emotional involvements. Moreover, in this play, unlike any other of Rowe's plays, all the conflict grows out of family relationships or out of the conflicts between personal and public honor and loyalty among friends and allies. There is no outside force of evil. Fate does not intervene. The plot line presents a series of highly dramatic situations, but all of them arise naturally out of the initial situation.

The chief motivation of the plot conflict is clear immediately with the revelation that Aribert, the king's brother, and Ethelinda are already secretly married; for Rowe again employs the device of the secret marriage, one he has used in *all* of his plays. Moreover, Ethelinda, the daughter of the fallen British chieftain Flavian, is a Christian; and Aribert, persuaded by her eloquence, has become a Christian also. For Aribert it is difficult to decide which will displease his brother Hengist, the king, more—Aribert's new-found faith or his new bride. The elder Hengist, the father of the present king and of Aribert, had feared just such an eventuality and had forced the brothers to swear allegiance to Woden and to vow never to take a wife among the Christians.

It would at first seem, therefore, that Aribert's marriage to Ethelinda and the conflict of Christianity with the Saxon god Woden would be enough to structure the plot incidents, but more complications are revealed almost at once. The Saxon kingdom is in great turmoil. The British king, Ambrosius, once Hengist's friend and ally, now calls for war and demands the return of Kent, a part of the land the Saxons won at the cost of many of their own warriors. Moreover, Offa, one of their own Saxon princes from Jutland, who brought "twice ten thousand warriors" to aid Hengist, now realizes that Hengist delays his promised marriage to Offa's sister Rodogune, a delay Offa finds intolerable.

Hengist's reluctance to fulfill his promise to wed Rodogune is explained by the fact that two days before the beginning of the play, he had come upon Ethelinda (already his brother's bride) while he was hunting in the forest and had immediately fallen passionately in love with her. She, refusing to respond to his startlingly unexpected attentions, was taken by force to the palace. When Hengist appears for the first time on the stage, he, like Aribert, is faced with an insoluble problem; for, having fallen in love with Ethelinda, he can no longer consider a political marriage. Confronted by Offa and Rodogune together, he is challenged to fight by Offa; and he is scorned and ridiculed by Rodogune, who declares she will never become his queen. Rodogune is, in fact, secretly in love with Aribert.

The difficult questions of love versus honor and personal preference versus the responsibilities of the king are discussed and decided with the help of Hengist's friend and advisor, Seofried. Hengist is so deeply involved in his own emotional preoccupation with Ethelinda that he misjudges the threat to his kingdom that Rodogune represents. He decides that he will make Aribert "the pledge of peace." He knows nothing of Aribert's secret marriage, and Aribert in turn knows nothing of Hengist's passionate love for Ethelinda. When Aribert is informed of the plan, he is horrified at his brother's request and, still unaware of the true situation, calls for Ethelinda. When Seofried brings Ethelinda forward, the whole dilemma is suddenly clarified. Their fear that Hengist will disapprove of their marriage because of Ethelinda's birth and their Christian faith has been augmented by the horrifying possibility that the king will force her to become his wife.

Act III begins with a soliloquy by Seofried in which he laments that "I would preserve 'em both, the royal Brothers." Ethelinda must escape from her confinement within the palace. With Seofried's help, she flees to the camp of the Britons; and Aribert is left to face his brother, the king. To gain time for Ethelinda's escape, Aribert promises to pretend a response to Rodogune that he in no way feels. Aribert hardly has made such a resolution to pretense before Rodogune appears, and their dialogue of courtly wit and counter wit begins, only to end abruptly when the king himself bursts in upon them, raging at the loss of Ethelinda. In the violent exchange that follows, everything becomes clear. The king has discovered Aribert's relationship with Ethelinda; and Rodogune now discovers not only the reason for the king's coolness to her but the even more distressing fact that Aribert can never be hers. From this scene until the end of the play, the double triangle must be reckoned with. In his anger, the king commands the guards to seize Aribert and to offer him as a human sacrifice to Woden.

Act IV opens with Aribert in the temple surrounded by the

priests of the heathen gods of the ancient Saxons. His soliloquy is at once a lyric of praise to nature and a lament about the dark mysteries of the implacable deities of his fathers. The night has been filled with "the groans of poor lamenting ghosts" and with "the wild fantastic measures" of the "bloody priests." But all the priests have not been plotting his bloody torture. One appears and hands him a message: Ethelinda has reached the camp of the Britons where her brother will help protect her—she is safe from Hengist at least.

Meantime, Ethelinda's safety, however precious it may be, does not deliver Aribert. Almost immediately after the message of her flight is received, Rodogune appears. She has come, she tells Aribert, "To curse your tyrant brother, and deplore/ Your youthful hopes, thus all untimely blasted" (II, 107). She would persuade him to forget Ethelinda, to escape with her, and to join her in her brother's camp. Aribert refuses. To her question "Dost thou not wish to live?" he replies "I cannot . . . I dare die. But dare not be oblig'd. I dare not owe/ What I can never render back" (II, 110). She cannot believe that he would choose Ethelinda in preference to her as she reluctantly admits her defeat, the king enters.

The scene that follows between the two brothers rises to the sharpest opposition. Aribert taunts Hengist with the knowledge that Ethelinda has arrived safely in the camp of the Britons; and the king, totally overcome with frustration and anger, orders the priest to "begin the rites and dye the hallow'd steel/ Deep in his Christian blood" (II, 113). But, before the priests can carry out their orders, Seofried bursts in to report to the king that "Destruction threatens in our frighted streets" (II, 113). As the shouts of battle are heard outside, the king hastens away, commanding the priest to kill Aribert; but the priest turns to Aribert and says, "Be chear'd, my Lord, . . . I am your slave. The King is fled, and with him all your dangers" (II, 114).

There can be no simple release for Aribert, however; the priest's act of kindness is not complete before Rodogune reappears. Not willing to lose Aribert in spite of his refusal to accept her proffered love, she would rescue him and have him for herself since she now has captured Ethelinda to use as a pawn. As she announces her prize triumphantly, her soldiers bring in Ethelinda; and the confrontation of Ethelinda and Rodogune provides more than enough material for drama. Rodogune, jealous to distraction, has no pity; and Aribert pleads for Ethelinda's life in vain. Rodogune cannot—will not—relent. Instead, she commands that both Ethelinda and Aribert be put to death.

Act V opens with Seofried's informing the king that Oswald, Aribert's most trusted friend, has fostered a confederacy with the Britons to release Aribert, a confederacy now becoming increasingly successful. The king must agree to make some compromise or face civil rebellion. Hengist agrees to compromise; but, left alone with Seofried, he resolves to betray Oswald and his soldiers by taking Ethelinda and fleeing. Thus, if he loses his crown, he will have won a more valuable prize. It is not to be.

The scene changes to the temple where Aribert and Ethelinda walk toward their destiny. Heaven is their hope; they will die together to be united for all eternity. While they speak to each other, Rodogune appears to be a witness to the death of her rival. Moreover, as part of her evil vengeance, she wants Aribert to witness the torture of Ethelinda by the priests. But Rodogune and Hengist have plotted in vain; their goddess Fortune is a fickle ally. Before Rodogune can carry out her cruelty, the king staggers in, fatally wounded. Forgiving Aribert and begging his eternal pardon, Hengist has Aribert and Ethelinda released and gives them his crown. Rodogune, subdued at last, agrees to depart; but she curses the lovers. Nonetheless, neither her curses nor Hengist's death destroys the happiness of Ethelinda and Aribert. In the concluding lines of the play, Oswald says:

> The winds shall scatter all those idle curses
> Far, far away from you, while every blessing
> Attends to crown you. From your happy nuptials,
> From Royal *Aribert* of *Saxon* race,
> Join'd to the fairest of the *British* dames,
> Methinks I read the people's future happiness;
> And *Britain* takes its pledge of peace from you.   (II, 128)

And Ethelinda, prophesying the future, says:

> Nor are those pious hopes of peace in vain;
> Since I have often heard a holy sage,
> . . . .
> Disclose the wonders of the time to come.
> Of royal race a British Queen shall rise,

Great, gracious, pious, fortunate and wise:
To distant lands she shall extend her fame,
And leave to latter times a mighty name:
Tyrants shall fall, and faithless Kings shall bleed,
And groaning nations by her arms be freed.
But chief this happy land her care shall prove,
And find from her a more than mother's love.
From hostile rage she shall preserve it free,
Safe in the compass of her ambient sea;
Tho fam'd her arms in many a cruel fight,
Yet most in peaceful arts she shall delight,
And her chief glory shall be to UNITE,
Picks, Saxons, Angles, shall no more be known,
But *Briton* be the noble name alone.
With joy their ancient hate they shall forego,
While discord hides her baleful head below:
Mercy, and truth, and right she shall maintain,
And ev'ry virtue crowd to grace her reign:
Auspicious Heav'n on all her days shall smile,
And with eternal UNION bless her *British* Isle.   (II, 128)

VIII   *The Political and Religious Ideas in* The Royal Convert

Johnson in his criticism of the play comments upon this conclusion by saying: "This play discovers its own date, by a prediction of
the *Union* in imitation of Cranmer's prophetick promises to *Henry
the Eighth*. The anticipated blessings of the union are not very
naturally introduced, nor very happily expressed."[12] Certainly the
ending seems to a twentieth-century reader unduly didactic and
dramatically awkward; but in November, 1707, the responses must
have been somewhat different.

Johnson, in fact, misreads the play in finding "anticipated blessings." The play is a strong plea for support for the union and an
equally vigorous statement of the value of Christianity; moreover, it
is not a prediction for the future; it quite precisely comments on the
two topics: the support of the union and universal Christianity—two
topics much debated between 1703 and 1707. While Rowe himself
had said in his Prologue that some would say "This Tragedy's such a
damn'd grave stuff," the events of the current economic and political
scene must have made his didacticism much more appropriate at
that time than it has been for later audiences. With *The Royal
Convert* in 1707, as in 1705 with *Ulysses,* Rowe has been consistent

in following his practice of writing in a conventional dramatic formula while supporting political and social ideas of his own. A review of some of the events of 1706–1707 will confirm our view.

The victory of Ramillies that occurred in May, 1706, brought new power for the English; it stopped the advance of the French in the Netherlands and allowed the English to set up the fortifications that were to insure the success of the Allies to free the Spanish Netherlands from French control. In September, 1706, the battle of Turin was won by Prince Eugene; and thus Louis XIV was stopped in Italy as well as in the Netherlands. In October, Barcelona fell to the Allies, and in the closing weeks of the year much of the eastern seaboard of Spain became theirs.[13] By the end of 1706, the Mediterranean area had been secured for the English, and Portugal had become one of England's most loyal friends. The Whigs were in control in the Parliament that convened in December, 1706; and its members, with Queen Anne herself supported by a grateful nation, did homage to John Churchill, the great Duke of Marlborough.[14]

When Queen Anne succeeded William III on March 8, 1702, she received, along with the approval of most of her English subjects, the tangled web of the problems that William had been involved with in Europe, especially those of the Alliance (a loose federation of Holland, the German states, and England united only in their opposition to France) which was determined to oppose and control the power of Louis XIV. But along with the problems, Anne also received the advice and loyalty of John Churchill, the Duke of Marlborough. She had, in fact, already had the friendship and support of both the Duke and his wife Sarah, her closest friend. In 1702, Marlborough was one of the most powerful figures in England. At the time of William's coming to England in 1688, he had been one of the chief organizers in the successful action against James II. And in the settlement of the succession on Princess Anne, now Queen Anne, he had been one of her staunch supporters. In August, 1704, two years after Anne became queen, Marlborough and the Allies defeated the French at the battle of Blenheim, a great victory celebrated in September with thanksgiving ceremonies at St. Paul's Cathedral by the queen and by a military march in January after Marlborough himself had returned to England. The victory of Ramillies two years later extended and reaffirmed the power of Marlborough and the Allies, and the success of the summer following it made 1706 something of an *annus mirabilis*.

Moreover, during the years 1705 and 1706 the whole interwoven tapestry of English politics, the war, and the attendant domestic policies to support the various threads of the struggle for British supremacy over Louis XIV began to make a visible pattern. Within this pattern the design of the Scottish thistle and its distinctive outline became increasingly evident. Since the days of James I (1603–25), the association between England and Scotland had been marred by disputes in both church and state; the time of William III (1689–1702) and Anne (1702–14) saw no conclusion to those disputes. Neither High Church Tories nor Whig Dissenters agreed with the Scots. According to one authority, "The Scot was either a Jacobite or a Presbyterian, and in either capacity he alienated four-fifths of English sympathy."[15] Moreover, economic conditions in Scotland were in a sorry state indeed. Much of the land was still as it had been in Anglo-Saxon days, and even those products that might have been traded were banned on the world market by England and her laws. However they might disagree among themselves, the Scots needed desperately to come to terms with the English.

In 1707, the union with Scotland was the most important event of national policy. George M. Trevelyan writing about it says: "It would be an error to suppose that the Union was passed in the reign of Anne because English and Scots were in a friendly mood. The opposite was the case. The badness of the terms on which the two nations were living was the motive of the Union. Statesmen on both sides of the Border saw the necessity of a union of the two Parliaments in one, as the only alternative to war, and as the only political machine strong enough to stand the shocks of the perpetually recurring antagonism of North and South Britain."[16]

Rowe was to have an intimate knowledge of the history of the union and of one of its most important advocates, when he became secretary in 1709 for the Duke of Queensberry, who in 1707 had played an important role in working out the terms of the union. And in 1707 the Parliament of Scotland (before the union independent of England) was chiefly concerned with the Protestant Succession and the War of the Spanish Succession, just as the English were. Closely allied with England in these two interests, the Scots were not allowed to share the profits of the English colonial trade; and it is small wonder that they harbored bitter resentment for their "South Briton" allies. As for the English, the Whigs saw quite clearly that, if Anne died before the war was won, Louis XIV and the Pretender might very well have a convenient back door through Scotland into victory in England. Beginning even in the winter of 1705, the winter *Ulysses* was presented, the negotiations for the union had taken on an urgent and desperate tone in England. The arguments about the Protestant Succession had assumed such proportion that some settlement had to be concluded. Unfortunately the whole complex discussion continued to be hampered by the unresolved problems of the English greed about trade and the Scots' bitter resentment in being excluded.

An important political business of the winter of 1705–06[17] and the spring of 1706 was the appointment of the Scottish Commissioners to be responsible for the terms of the union. Queensberry, Rowe's future employer, played a key role in drawing up the proposals, and with his help the Treaty was passed in the Scottish Estates by February, 1707. It was debated in Parliament and agreed upon. On May 1, 1707, the Union Treaty became official and the queen again gave thanks at St. Paul's for another victory.

In an estimate of the time that followed the Union Treaty, Trevelyan says: ". . . the new yoke, though it galled, held fast; and if prosperity came late, it was one day to come in full plenty as a direct result of the Union. Meanwhile the immediate object of the statesmen who had united the Parliament was fulfilled upon Anne's death: the House of Hanover succeeded to the throne of Great Britain, and no rival reigned at Holyrood."[18]

On this May day of victory celebration Rowe's association with Queensberry was still in the future at a time when the old animosities between Scotland and England had reappeared and Queensberry had been forced to be mediator between them. In his two plays, *Ulysses* and *The Royal Convert*, however, Rowe's awareness of the situation is clearly evident. We have seen how Rowe offers in *Ulysses* a graceful tribute to Queen Anne; in *The Royal Convert*, he makes a plea for peace between brothers and a union of all England, a union consummated, moreover, in the Christian faith. Like the earlier *Ulysses*, *The Royal Convert* does not conform to a strict allegorical pattern. Instead, from the first, the confusions and conflicts of the play speak in broad and general "lessons."

But, when the lessons are read together, the point is clear that the kingdom must be united, Kent must be a part of the larger Britain, and this union must be achieved without the help of foreign allies. Neither Hengist nor Aribert could tolerate Rodogune, no matter what their response to each other in their rivalry over Ethelinda might be. Their regard for Rodogune is never anything more than the diplomatic politeness of courtly conduct. Even in reply to her curse at the end of the play, Aribert's speech is a gracious acknowledgment of her power; but it is not in any sense an acknowledgment of any possible role she might have had in the kingdom. A united Britain ruled by a Christian king and his queen can be the only happy conclusion of the tragic complications that Rowe designed for his play; and its parallel must have been clear to his audience. In Ethelinda's devotion to her religion and in her unfailing loyalty to its power and teaching, Rowe's audience must also have been reminded of their own Anne, whose devotion to the church was a constant factor in English political affairs throughout her reign. Always jealous of her prerogative as the head of the Church of England, she was painfully sensitive to any criticism that indicated any failure on her part in ecclesiastical matters.

The months immediately preceding the production of *The Royal Convert* were particularly trying ones for Anne and her government. The war did not make notable progress in the summer campaign of 1707. In reality, the Allies lost important opportunities to bring about peace. The Duke of Marlborough and the Whigs were becoming more and more alienated from Anne, while she became more and more involved with the High Tories. Indeed, Trevelyan says that from the autumn of 1707 "party government in the strict sense of the word established itself . . . ."[19] From late summer through the fall and winter, the chief point of conflict centered around appointments in the church—Anne was determined to have her way in the appointment of two Tory Bishops; and the Whigs in power were equally set against her. Eventually, a compromise was reached, but not until the country was reminded again of how strong was the bond between church and state—at least the state as ruled by Anne.[20]

In *The Royal Convert*, the religious question plays a major part from the beginning of the play. Aribert's opening revelation of his secret marriage to Ethelinda is made in the confession of his own conversion to Christianity. His faithful Oswald, willing to tolerate Ethelinda's faith, is chiefly concerned with "how will the King and our fierce Saxon chiefs/ Approve his bride and faith," and his advice to Aribert is to

> Be cautious of your danger, rest in silence.
> In holy matters, zeal may be your guide,

And lift you on her flaming wings to Heav'n;
But here on earth trust reason, and be safe.   (II, 78)

Ethelinda does not appear upon the stage until the middle of the
second act when, accompanied by the king's henchman, Seofried,
she enters weeping, declaring in her first speech "That power in
whom I trust will set me free" (II, 90). She calls upon heaven:
"Guard me, thou gracious Heaven,/ Thou that has been my sure
defence till now,/ Guard me from Hell, and that its blackest crime"
(II, 90). Aribert would insure the safety of their secret marriage by
killing Seofried, the only witness to their secret; but Ethelinda will
not allow him to do so. When Seofried declares he will aid and guard
them, not betray them, she declares her faith in the face of peril:

'Tis terrible! my fears are mighty on me,
And all the coward woman trembles in me.
But oh! when hope and never-failing faith
Revive my fainting soul, and lift my thoughts
Up to yon' azur sky, and burning lights above.
Methinks I see the warlike host of Heav'n
Radiant in glitt'ring arms, and beamy gold,
The great Angelic pow'rs go forth by bands,
To succour truth and innocence below.
Hell trembles at the sight, and hides its head
In utmost darkness, while on earth each heart,
Like mine, is fill'd with peace and joy unutterable.   (II, 93–94)

When at the end of the scene they must part, Ethelinda again
calls upon her faith—this time to reassure Aribert:

Oh lift thy eyes up to that holy pow'r,
Whose wond'rous truths, and Majesty divine,
Thy Ethelinda taught thee first to know;
There fix thy faith, and triumph o'er the world;
For who can help, or who can save besides?
Does not the deep grow calm, and the rude North
Be hush'd at his command? thro' all his works,
Does not his servant Nature hear his voice?
Hear and obey? Then what is impious man
That we should fear him, when Heav'n owns our cause?   (II, 95)

When the king discovers that Ethelinda has indeed escaped from
his imprisonment and that she is, moreover, already his brother's

wife, he accuses Aribert of being "False to our Gods, as to thy King and brother" (II, 104). Aribert's reply, like Ethelinda's witness, is a serious tribute to the Christian faith:

> —'tis my glory that the Christian light
> Has dawn'd like day, upon my darker mind,
> And taught my soul the noblest use of reason!
> Taught her to soar aloft, to search, to know,
> That vast eternal fountain of her being;
> Then warm with indignation, to despise
> The things you call our country's Gods, to scorn
> And trample on their ignominious altars.   (II, 104)

In sharp contrast is his heathen brother's command:

> Hear, and be present to my justice, hear me,
> While thus I vow to your offended Deities
> This traitor's life; he dies, nor ought on earth
> Saves his devoted head. One to the priests:
> Bid them be swift, and dress their bloody altars
> With every circumstance of tragic pomp:
> To-day a royal victim bleeds upon them.
> Rich shall the smoak and steaming gore ascend,
> To glut the vengeance of our angry Gods.   (II, 105)

During the scenes with Rodogune, Aribert pleads that his love for Ethelinda is greater than his love of life. But, in the last act when he and Ethelinda are led into the temple by the priest, Ethelinda combines their love with the love of heaven in the proper Christian manner. Indeed, the whole scene, set out in dialogue between Ethelinda and Aribert, is the Christian resignation of the individual's will and wish to the will and providence of God. Ethelinda concludes by saying:

> If our dear hopes,
> If what we value most on earth, our loves,
> Are blasted thus by death's untimely hand,
> If nothing good remains for us below,
> So much the rather let us turn our thoughts,
> To seek beyond the stars our better portion;
> That wond'rous bliss which Heav'n reserves in store,
> Well to reward us for our losses here;
> Which shall be more to thee than Ethelinda,

And more to me—Oh vast excess of happiness!
Where shall my soul make room for more than Aribert?   (II, 123)

Rodogune's intrusion is that of the cruel heathen princess indeed.
She orders their death; and, as the scene is drawn following
Rodogune's commands, the inner part of the temple is shown with a
fire already burning on one of the altars, near which are knives,
axes, and other instruments of torture. But death has no terror for
the Christians, for, as Ethelinda says, "The free, impassive soul
mounts on the wing, Beyond the reach of racks, and tort'ring
flames,/ And scorns their tyranny" (II, 125). Nor does she have to
prove her courage. It is Hengist, the king, who dies—not the
lovers—and his are bitter words as he is wounded and falls at
Ethelinda's feet saying,

> . . . those envious gods
> Have done their worst, and blasted all my hopes;
> They have despoil'd me of my crown and life, . . .
> Thee—they have robb'd me of my joys in thee—
> Have trod me down to wither in the grave.—   (II, 126)

With the death of Hengist and with the happy release of the two
Christians, only Rodogune remains to represent the evils of the
heathen worship; and even she prays to nature to ask justice to "Let
woman once be mistress in her turn,/ Subdue mankind beneath her
haughty scorn, And smile to see the proud oppressor mourn" (II,
128). Since her prayer is followed by the speech about the union,
the final impression of the play is a tribute to Anne both as head of
the church and as queen of the nation, a nice and graceful combination of the themes of the play.

Rowe's precise comments about the Union Treaty and his direct
and forceful support of Christianity and the church are strikingly
underscored in *The Royal Convert,* especially when we remember
that England under Queen Anne made no division between church
and state. Contrary to Johnson's view, the "anticipated blessings"
are "happily expressed" in our view of the play.

CHAPTER 7

Jane Shore: *A Play*
"to rouse the passions"

IN 1714, seven years after *The Royal Convert*, Rowe presented his next play, *Jane Shore*, his best and most successful tragedy. In the years following *The Royal Convert* (1707) Rowe had been engaged in a variety of tasks both public and private. In 1709, he had become secretary to the Duke of Queensberry, a post he held until the Duke's death in 1711; and in 1709 his edition of Shakespeare was published, work that must have engaged him for several months prior to its appearance. In the year before, 1708, he had appealed to the public to send to his publisher Jacob Tonson any materials on the life of Shakespeare it might possess. His friend Betterton had collected information about Shakespeare for several years; and, at Rowe's request, he collaborated with him on the life prefixed to the first volume of *The Works of Mr. William Shakespear*.[1]

This edition of Shakespeare insured Rowe at least a footnote in twentieth-century literary scholarship. In his own era, his publication was an elegant and welcome addition to a gentleman's library. If by later standards Rowe's work was little more than seeing through the press a reprint of the fourth folio edition of Shakespeare, it was because neither Rowe nor his world understood modern editorial methods that require the collation of all extant texts to establish an authoritative one. Rowe was, however, the first editor who divided the texts into scenes and acts and who made a list of the characters that preceded each play. The edition of 1709 was followed by a second in 1714, and its title page announces that the work is "Adorn'd with Cuts." These "Cuts" are engravings depicting various scenes from the plays, illustrations ranging from pictures of the storm scenes of *Lear* and *The Tempest* to ones of the elaborately furnished and decorated rooms of *The Taming of the Shrew* and the opulence of Desdamona's bedroom in *Otello*. These engravings added significantly to the design of an edition, that provided the public with an easy access to Shakespeare.

In these years between *The Royal Convert* and *Jane Shore* Rowe had, moreover, continued to do translations and to write a variety of political and occasional verse. In 1707, he published a translation of the *Golden Verses of Pythagoras* and a pamphlet poem entitled *On the Late Glorious Success of Her Majesty's Arms*. A translation of Nicholas Boileau's *Lutrin . . . render'd into English Verse. To Which is prefixed some account of Boileau's Writings and of this Translation by N. Rowe* was published in 1708. Some of the work during this time Rowe shared with other, less well known writers; and, since his publishers used his name as advertisement, he thereby helped to sell the books and to keep his own fame before the public.[2] Rowe's writing during 1709–1711, when he served as secretary to the Duke of Queensbury, was largely poetry of "wit" to friends or topical verse about current affairs.[3]

In 1714, when *Jane Shore* was being readied for production, Rowe's own public and private situation was quite different from that in 1707 when he had given his tribute to Queen Anne and the Union Treaty with Scotland in *The Royal Convert*. He had learned firsthand about the affairs of state as the Duke's secretary; in 1709, he had added fame as the editor of Shakespeare to his reputation as a dramatist; and he had lent his name to various translations.

Jane Shore was produced at the Theatre Royal in Drury Lane on February 2, 1714. By early eighteenth-century standards it was very successful, paying fifteen times in February and three in March. Rowe was given three benefit nights; and Mrs. Oldfield, who created the role of Jane Shore, was given a benefit on March 1. In addition to the profit from the play, Rowe received fifty pounds, fifteen shillings, from Lintott for the publication of the book.

I *Prologue to the Play*

Jane Shore is a remarkable and memorable play. Rowe's own Prologue to it acknowledges its concern with native tradition in the first four lines, which read:

> Tonight, if you have brought your good old taste,
> We'll treat you with a downright English feast,

> A tale, which told long since in homely wise,
> Hath never fail'd of melting gentle eyes.

These two themes, "the good old taste . . . a downright English feast" and "A tale . . . that/ Hath never fail'd of melting gentle eyes," interwoven with Rowe's polished verse, comprise the play. As we have already seen, Rowe had from the very beginning resorted to such themes for his special interest; but he refined them in *Jane Shore* in such a way that they served the ends of true tragedy. Invoking the memory of Shakespeare himself, Rowe establishes his intent when he says he has in these scenes "made it more his care/ To rouse the passions, than to charm the ear."

In *Ulysses* and in *The Royal Convert*, Rowe had retained the characteristics proper for the heroic drama of his predecessors in that he had grafted upon the old roots the new plants of pathos and patriotism, but in neither play was he entirely successful. He had taken the Homeric epic and made it in *Ulysses* into an Augustan domestic tragedy with a patriotic tribute to the queen and a tragic subplot of young love in the story of Telemachus and Semanthe. In *The Royal Convert*, he had used Britain's early history to set forth the "lessons" of union and of Christian Providence. But *Ulysses* necessarily remains the familiar tale of Ulysses' return, and *The Royal Convert* remains remote in time and place. The flowers produced from such grafts were beautiful but short lived.

In *Jane Shore*, Rowe succeeded in creating a new flower sturdily produced from its own roots by using actual historical figures and by adapting historical events to his own purpose—people and events, moreover, from a time in English history very like his own in its divided loyalties to the crown and in its shifting class lines. There is still some of the heroic in *Jane Shore*, but it is now in terms of a native historical style that can naturally become the medium for the theme of patriotism. In selecting the story of Jane Shore, Rowe made a fortunate choice because Jane herself was already a popular historical figure to Rowe's audience; and she became in his hands the epitome of the sinner-saint, a creation he made to fit a unique pattern of his own.

Jane Shore was the daughter of a textile merchant and the wife of a goldsmith, she had been chosen by King Edward VI to be his mistress because of her beauty and her wit; and she had been an admired and envied figure at court as well as in the streets of London for some years prior to Edward's death. Sir Thomas More's moving account of her beauty and her kindness in his *History of King Richard III* (ca. 1513) was the first of many versions of her story, for she was still alive when he wrote of her. More recounts her charities and repeats the steps of her downfall when, after Edward's death, she became the mistress of Thomas Grey, first Marquess of Dorset, and perhaps the mistress of William, Lord Hastings, as well. She was accused by Richard III of being a sorceress and used by Richard to accuse Hastings. Hastings was executed; and Jane was forced to do public penance by walking barefoot through the streets, with a burning taper in hand to St. Paul's. In the years after her death she became a favorite example for writers engaged in contrasting beauty to virtue. Shakespeare made reference to her in his *Richard III*; Thomas Churchyard wrote *Complaint of Shore's Wife*; and Michael Drayton wrote *An Epistle of Mistress Shore to King Edward the Fourth*.[4] To Rowe's audience, then, Jane's story was no new and surprising tale of exotic peoples or places.

The setting of *Jane Shore* in London made it thoroughly English, as did the political complications of the situation. Moreover, Rowe's selections from the materials he had at hand are interesting because of the way in which he arranges them for the variations he is most skillful in producing. In *Jane Shore* we find again situations similar to those of the earlier plays—the fair but distressed heroine, who gives too much for love; the courtier who uses passion to tempt the frail heroine to destruction but, failing in that, uses brutal force in attempted rape; the usurping tyrant, who serves as the instrument of evil to bring about the catastrophe of tragedy; the friendship, which should serve in the interest of the fair one but does not; and, finally, the fatality of injured beauty with its consequent tragic loss in a world so overcome with evil that it can no longer support the saint but must demand justice of the sinner.

In handling the plot of *Jane Shore*, Rowe is much simpler and more direct than he had been in the earlier plays. In the exposition, he presents, one after the other, the major complications of the situation; but the presentation is so skillfully done that neither artificiality nor awkwardness exist as in the exposition in *The Fair Penitent*. Although Rowe does not match Shakespeare in subtlety, he has evidently profited from his study of the techniques of the master. By the end of the first act, we know that Jane Shore, having been mistress to Edward IV, has fallen into a lamentable state since

his death; that Richard of Gloucester would become king whatever
the expense; that William, Lord Hastings, while he is willing to sue
Gloucester on behalf of Jane, will not compromise his devotion to
Edward's children; that Alicia, while she thinks of herself as Jane's
closest friend, cannot admit any interference in her jealous posses-
sion of Hastings; and, finally, that Jane herself wishes nothing of her
present world but an opportunity to repent and return to a simple
goodness.

Whatever the influence of Shakespeare's *Richard III* and of
Shakespeare's handling of plot and character, Rowe's play is his own
from the first; his characters are his and his emphasis on theme. The
role of Gloucester, who became Richard III, is the chief focus for
Shakespeare; and Hastings has the chief supporting role. In *Jane
Shore*, both Gloucester and Hastings are only used in supporting
roles to that of Jane, who in reality dominates the play from the
beginning.[5] Thus the emphasis is turned from kings and nobles to
"A nymph forsaken, and a perjur'd swain," as Rowe says in his
Prologue.

II *The Opening Situation*

The incidents of the play are quite simple; and they focus, as they
should, almost wholly on Jane, the central character. However,
since she has been the king's mistress, the political situation is as
important as her personal circumstances; and, since the traditions of
history had already given Rowe the development of the plot, he
merely had to add the pathos. The play opens at the Tower of
London with a scene in which Richard of Gloucester and his friends,
Sir Richard Ratcliffe and Catesby, explore their political situation.
As is quickly evident, Hastings opposes Gloucester, who is, as
Catesby says, "One of the stubborn sort." Moreover, Gloucester
adds, "And yet this tough impracticable heart/ Is govern'd by a
dainty-finger'd girl." Ratcliffe makes the meaning clear by commenting that "The fair Alicia,/ Of noble birth and exquisite of
feature,/ Has held him long a vassal to her beauty" (II, 140). Shortly
thereafter, Hastings himself, entering alone, speaks not of Alicia but
of Jane's plight. Her lands have been seized; and he, Hastings,
would have the deed rectified. The two, Gloucester and Hastings,
will determine Jane's destiny in the public world of the court; but
Jane will make her own decision in her private world.

The scene shifts from the noble lords to Jane's house. Bellmour, her neighbor, entertains a friend, Dumont, who, as we soon discover, is Shore, Jane's former husband, who has arrived to seek her out. As the three of them—Jane, Bellmour, and Dumont—converse, Alicia enters. She is Jane's friend, as well as Hasting's mistress. Together, they all talk of times past as lost from the present. Jane is completely changed. She is no longer tempted by the favors of the noble or rich; truly repentant, she would not only confess her transgressions but she would set right the king's legacy—she would support his widowed queen and her sons. Jane's melancholy beauty and her sweetness in this first scene with Alicia establish the major features of her character.

In contrast to Jane, Alicia is excitable and voluble; and she is unwilling to believe Jane's gloomy predictions about the future. She begs her to "Exert thy charms, seek out the stern protector, [Gloucester]/ And sooth his savage temper with thy beauty" (II, 145). But Jane will have nothing to do with such a suggestion, for she feels that she has lost her beauty and lives always with grief. She declares her friendship to Alicia and asks her to take and keep for her a casket of jewels—her last security against complete poverty. And, even though Alicia has already noticed Hastings' interest in Jane, she accepts the jewels and pledges her eternal devotion.

III   *The Complication of Passion*

In the second act, Rowe develops Jane's inevitable story. Hastings arrives to report Gloucester's willingness to give Jane an audience; unhappily, Hastings must speak first with Alicia: for, no matter how much he would avoid her, he cannot. Their confrontation is one of violence. When Hastings does speak shortly thereafter with Jane, he gives his message of Gloucester's mercy; and, for his own reward, Hastings would have her as a mistress, not as a supplicant. Jane's reply is simple and direct: "Never! by those chaste lights above, I swear,/ My soul shall never know pollution more;/ Forbear, my Lord!—Here let me rather die" (II, 153).

The drama of the ensuing struggle in which Jane resists Hastings and he attempts to force her is brief, far briefer than such scenes in Rowe's earlier tragedies and far more naturally and simply constructed. Dumont (Shore), hearing Jane's cries, comes to her aid; and, in the swordplay that follows, he disarms Hastings but refuses to kill him. For his thanks, Hastings says, "Curse on my failing hand! your better fortune/ Has given you 'vantage o'er me; but perhaps/ Your triumph may be bought with dear repentance" (II, 154). Jane knows at once the meaning of such a threat; but Dumont, not disturbed by Hastings's threats, speaks only to Jane herself: "Fear not, my worthiest mistress; 'tis a cause,/ In which Heaven's guard shall wait you" (II, 155). And when Dumont continues, he urges Jane to flee the court "Where innocence is sham'd, and blushing modesty/ Is made the scorner's jest." Jane can think of no way to escape. Indeed there is no way of escape for her or for Dumont. Act II ends with Dumont's speech on the virtues of retirement, but we later learn from Jane that Dumont "Was seiz'd on by the cruel hand of pow'r/ Forc'd from my house, and borne away to prison" (II, 157).

IV   *The Results of Uncontrolled Passion*

The third act opens as Alicia enters holding a paper in her hand. She is alone; and she reveals in her soliloquy not only her plan to avenge the wrong she feels but also her motives. She will accuse Jane of being the cause of Hastings's refusal to "pluck the Crown from Edward's infant brow." Moreover, she clearly recognizes that her own jealousy has ended her friendship with Jane. When Jane appears, however, she is so overwrought with her concern and her total involvement in her own sorrows that she allows Alicia to betray her. Jane has a paper in hand to give to Gloucester as he passes by, a paper she gives Alicia to read. As Alicia pretends to read it, she substitutes her own letter for Jane's and hands it to Gloucester as he comes in with his friends, Sir Richard Ratcliff, Catesby, and other courtiers and attendants. Gloucester already acts the role of king. Alicia's letter of accusation of Jane's influence over Hastings is precisely the means Gloucester seeks to entrap Hastings.

Seemingly unaware of his own danger, Hastings is the more easily caught. Coming upon Gloucester and his friends, Hastings begins to discuss Jane's position, to speak of Jane's devotion to Edward's sons, of his interest in her and of Alicia's relation to him—but, when Gloucester turns to a discussion of the crown, Hastings is forced to speak of the "deadly heart of faction" that can divide and spoil the land.[6] While they talk of her, Jane appears, and Gloucester seems to offer his protection to her and Dumont. Her humble thanks to him are made in reference to her past—both her offenses and her kindness; for Jane declares what all know to be true—that she never forgot the widow's want or the orphan's cry. Gloucester does not reply to her defense; instead, he begins to accuse her of disloyalty to him; speaking to her in measured terms, he tells her:

> The state, for many high and potent reasons,
> Deeming my brother *Edward's* sons unfit
> For the imperial weight of England's crown—
> Therefore have resolv'd
> To set aside their unavailing infancy,
> And vest the sov'reign rule in abler hands.
> This, tho' of great importance to the public,
> Hastings, for very peevishness and spleen,
> Does stubbornly oppose. (II, 165)

Jane exclaims, "Does he! does Hastings!"; and, immediately perceiving the implications for Hastings, she calls upon heaven to "Save him from wrong, adversity, and shame," and begins to lament for "The poor forsaken, royal little ones!" (II, 166). The mounting tension of the scene underscores Jane's generous and loyal nature and Gloucester's single-minded purpose to mount the throne.[7]

In this whole conversation between Gloucester and Jane, Rowe has skillfully played one theme against another in his contrapuntal treatment of patriotism and love: Gloucester would use Jane's beauty and what he presumes to be her relationship with Hastings for the fulfillment of his own personal objective; Jane, suing for his mercy for herself and Dumont, would use his power to restore justice and to support virtue.

As the counterturn comes in Gloucester's explicit accusation against Hastings, Jane's response to the injustice offered Hastings is generous and admirable. Whatever Hastings's demands upon her personally, she responds to his fierce, unyielding loyalty to Edward and his sons. She will not be moved by any of Gloucester's threats; and, when he pronounces her doom, she humbly submits. Richard of Gloucester's punishment is fearful indeed:

> Go some of you, and turn this strumpet forth;
> Spurn her into the street, there let her perish,
> And rot upon a dunghill. Thro' the city
> See it proclaim'd, That none, on pain of death,
> Presume to give her comfort, food, or harbour;
> Who ministers the smallest comfort, dies.
> Her house, her costly furniture, and wealth,

> The purchase of her loose luxurious life,
> We seize on for the profit of the state.
> Away! be gone!   (II, 167)

In her reply, Jane recognizes that her past offenses must be reckoned and accounted for:

> O thou most righteous judge—
> Humbly, behold, I bow myself to thee,
> And own thy justice in this hard decree:
> No longer then my ripe offences spare,
> But what I merit let me learn to bear.
> Yet since 'tis all my wretchedness can give,
> For my past crimes for forfeit life receive;
> No pity for my suff'rings here I crave,
> And only hope forgiveness in the grave.   (II, 167)

As the scene and her speech come to an end, Jane has become the
saint indeed. If, in her conversation earlier with Hastings, she has
shown her true repentance not only in being sorry for her sins but
also in refusing to be tempted again, she has at the conclusion of Act
IV made her martyrdom certain. She does so in terms of her loyalty
and patriotism to her country as much as for her former love for
Edward. Gloucester calls her strumpet, but he calls vengeance on
her, not for her former deeds, but because he cannot command her
to join him in his own evil purpose. The themes of love and loyalty,
jealousy and ambition, passion and reason have all come together.
Act V does not extend the fugue; it simply resolves it to its inevitable
conclusion.

Jane is taken away, but her departure does not end the action; for,
although the drama is hers, she cannot complete the themes alone,
just as Gloucester's ambition is not enough to resolve the issues
either. The council waits outside, and Hastings is among their
number. In fact, Hastings, who has believed Gloucester's declaration of pity for Jane and friendship for him, has fallen so completely
into Gloucester's evil plan that he listens attentively as Gloucester
closes the trap upon him. Gloucester asks the council's advice for
"What punishment your wisdom shall think meet/ T' inflict upon
those damnable contrivers,/ Who shall with potions, charms, and
witching drugs,/ Practice against our person and our life" (II, 168).
Hastings suggests that the punishment be death; the accusation is

against Hastings himself. As proof of the "damnable contrivers," Gloucester shows his withered arm—he stretches it out to accuse Hastings, calls him an "audacious traitor," and places him with the queen and Jane among those who have put a curse upon him.

The melodrama of this scene would be excessive had we not already known about Gloucester's resolution to have the crown at any cost. The suddenness of his doom to Hastings. Hasting's own innocent support of the verdict, followed immediately by his stunned and simple speech, all make the action believable. Turning to Ratcliffe, Hastings says: "What! and no more but this—how, to the scaffold!/ Oh gentle Ratcliffe! tell me, do I hold thee?/ Or if I dream, what shall I do to wake, . . ." (II, 169). Hastings is—indeed has been—a brave man, fearless in battle; death must come to all men; and he must accept what he cannot change. He will "die as a man should," but his ordeal is not over; and our sympathy increases for him when Alicia appears to reproach him as she says: "Thy cruel scorn has stung me to the heart and set my burning bosom all in flames" (II, 170). To Jane, he had abandoned reason for passion; but Alicia's loss of reason is the jealousy of madness.

Alicia recounts to him her revenge on Jane, never thinking that her loss of Hastings would result from it—she begs his pity and forgiveness for "the fatal rashness of ungovern'd love." In his speeches that follow, Hastings, like Jane, becomes a sinner-saint: he admits guilt, asks pardon, and prays that Alicia's "Good angels visit thy aflictions,/ And bring thee peace and comfort from above." His redemption has been achieved through his evocation of reason when he says to Alicia,

> 'Tis all in vain, this rage that tears thy bosom
> Like a poor bird that flutters in its cage,
> Thou beats thyself to death.   (II, 173)

And his final speech to her seeks to help her to goodness:

> I charge thee by our present common miseries,
> By our past loves, if yet they have a name,
> By all thy hopes of peace here and hereafter,
> Let not the rancour of thy hate pursue
> The innocence of thy unhappy friend.   (II, 173)

But Alicia will never become the sinner-saint; she closes the act with a curse far more damning then any Hastings had spoken to Jane. She is already beyond redemption.

Act V belongs entirely to Jane—to Jane as she becomes more and more abandoned and pathetic, as she becomes more and more the martyred saint. By the end of the fourth act, Rowe has already resolved the major complications of his plot: Jane has resisted Hastings, has felt the consequences of Alicia's jealousy, and has suffered for her loyalty to the young king. Her remaining possessions have been confiscated, Hastings has been beheaded, and Alicia has gone mad. Therefore, from this point, the resolution of the action is brief. When Jane comes to seek help from Alicia, she is turned away. Left alone, she is near collapsing when Shore and Bellmour appear. Through Bellmour, she is reunited with Shore; but the reunion is brief because the guards seize both Bellmour and Shore. Jane cannot now part from Shore, and their touching farewells bring to an end the incidents of the drama. She dies, Shore is taken away by the guards, and Bellmour concludes the play by saying:

> Let those who view this sad example, know,
> What fate attends the broken marriage vow;
> And teach their children in succeeding times,
> No common vengeance waits upon these crimes. (II, 185)

V *In Defense of Women*

In *Jane Shore*, Rowe gave his most moving demonstration of the position of women in the early eighteenth century—a demonstration that continued to be valid for over a century. From the opening situation of the play to its conclusion, the women, especially Jane Shore and Alicia, are a part of the complications of the political situation. In the opening scene, Gloucester is pleased that he has overcome his brother's queen when he says in the first line of the play, "Thus far success attends upon our counsels,/ And each event has answer'd to my wish;/ The Queen and all her upstart race are quell'd;" and it must surely have been clear to everyone that he was correct when he announced, that "The scepter and the golden wreath of royalty/ Seem hung within my reach" (II, 139). Moreover, with the mention of Hasting's opposition to Gloucester and his relationship to Alicia, we have both Gloucester, who manipulates all women, and Hastings, who desires all women, set in their respective roles—Gloucester will play out his excessive ambitions as a tyrant who attains his ends by whatever means are made available to him; Hastings, staunchly loyal to Edward and his sons, has a tragic weakness—his passions override his reason. Their relationships with Jane and Alicia reveal their characters.

In the beginning, Hastings has no awareness of the degree to which he will become involved with Jane's fortunes; he merely sees her as beautiful and desirable. Speaking of her melancholy fall from greatness, he gives proof of Jane's own speech later in the play about her plight as a woman, a speech for all the frail beauties of all time when she says,

> Why should I think that man will do for me
> What yet he never did for wretches like me?
> Mark by what partical justice we are judg'd;
> Such is the fate unhappy women find,
> And such the curse intail'd upon our kind,
> That man, the lawless libertine, may rove,
> Free and unquestion'd through the wilds of love;
> While woman, sense and nature's easy fool,
> If poor weak woman swerve from virtue's rule,
> If strongly charm'd, she leave the thorny way,
> And in the softer paths of pleasure stray;
> Ruin ensues, reproach and endless shame,
> And one false step entirely damns her fame.
> In vain look back on what she was before,
> She sets, like stars that fall, to rise no more.
>   (II, 146–147)

From Rowe's first play, *The Ambitious Step-Mother*, he had examined the position of women. Artemisa in *The Ambitious Step-Mother* has the qualities and virtues of an ambitious statesman, but she uses her beauty as a woman to achieve false ends. Jane, on the other hand, is the victim of her fatal beauty and sweetness. Rowe never lets us forget that she had indeed transgressed, but in this speech her gentle complaint of the consequences of being a beautiful and desirable woman heightens our sensibilities and makes us respond with pity for her weakness.

By modern standards, Alicia's is a very unsympathetic part. She raves and rants like a mad woman—indeed, she becomes mad at the end of the play. She is the epitome of unmotivated jealousy and its results on those innocent ones who inadvertently come in contact with it. As a frail, weak woman, Alicia commands no terror; and, in her position as Hasting's mistress, she can plead no virtue wronged because she is clearly an adulteress. Nevertheless, despite her unkindness to Jane, she is to be pitied; and in her speeches Rowe shows his sympathetic interest in the inequality of the woman's position.

Alicia feels that she has given everything to Hastings only to have him receive her with scorn; through the eighteenth century, and long after, if a woman gave away her virtue she could never again demand any response from a man—not love, not loyalty, certainly not fidelity or respect. Hastings feels that she demands more than he can give. When he declares his freedom from her, Alicia not only rages and rails at him but also pronounces a curse upon him. He shows no fear of her curse, only fear for "the fury of that tongue." And her imprecations merely serve to prompt his speech condemning all women:

> How fierce a fiend is passion? With what wildness,
> Why tyranny untam'd, it reigns in woman!
> Unhappy sex! Whose easy yielding temper
> Gives way to ev'ry appetite alike;
> Each gust of inclination, uncontrol'd
> Sweeps thro' their souls, and sets them in an uproar;
> Each motion of the heart rises to fury,
> And love in their weak bosoms is a rage
> As terrible as hate, and as destructive,   (II, 150–51)

When Alicia realizes that, in revenging her loss of Hastings by betraying Jane, she has in fact condemned him to death, she becomes completely mad. When Jane comes to her for help, she is already beyond reason as, calling Hastings's name, she says, "Oh my *Hastings*/ See his pale bloody head shoots glaring by me! Give him me back again, thou soft deluder,/ Thou beauteous witch—" (II, 179). She taunts Jane by reminding her of "All the smiling train of Courtiers,/ That bent the knee before thee"; and, when Jane cries "Oh! for Mercy!," she repeats the word:

> Mercy! I know it not—for I am miserable.
> I'll give thee misery, for here she dwells;

> This is her house, where the sun never dawns,
> The bird of night sits screaming o'er the roof,
> Grim spectres sweep along the horrid gloom,
> And nought is heard but wailings and lamentings.
> Hark! something cracks above; it shakes, it totters!
> And see the nodding ruin falls to crush me!
> 'Tis fall'n, 'tis here! I feel it on my brain! (II, 180)

Totally disoriented, Alicia thinks a "waving flood of blueish fire" envelops her; she feels she is drowning in the blood from the headless trunk of Hastings that beckons to her as she runs screaming off the stage followed by her servants. Rowe's use of the bizarre was never more effective than it is here. The contrast between Alicia's frightening, devil-possessed flight and Jane's merciful prayer as she goes reinforces our pity for Jane.

VI *Shore as Merciful Judge*

The role of Dumont-Shore is of paramount importance in establishing the themes of the play. The audience has known from the beginning that Dumont is Shore and that he has been watching Jane with growing compassion. But exactly what part he will serve in the tragic conclusion of Jane's story is a question. In his heroic defense of her when she refuses Hastings's unwelcome attention, he becomes her champion. In Act V, when he listens to the description of his friend Bellmour's account of Jane's public penance, our knowledge of his true identity heightens our sympathy for both Jane and him. This passage about the procession is a masterpiece of descriptive verse; and set, as it is, in the dramatic context of Jane's recent courageous refusal to bow to the tyranny of Gloucester, the whole scene assumes added significance. Jane has walked barefoot, her hair hanging loose, a burning taper in her hand, to stand in solemn penance at a public cross. Bellmour's account is moving indeed:

> I met her as returning
> In solemn penance from the public cross:
> Before her, certain racial officers,
> Slaves in authority, the knaves of Justice,
> Proclaim'd the *tyrant Gloster's* cruel orders.
> On either side her march'd an ill-look'd priest,
> Who, with severe, with horrid haggard eyes,
> Did ever and anon by turns upbraid her,

And thunder in her trembling ear damnation.
Around her, numberless the rabble flow'd,
Shouldring each other, crowding for a view,
Gaping and gazing, taunting and reviling;
Some pitying, but those, alas! how few!
The most, such iron hearts we are, and such
The base barbarity of human kind,
With insolence and leud reproach pursu'd her,
Hooting and railing, and with villainous hands
Gath'ring the filth from out the common ways
To hurl upon her head.
. . . .
Feeble she seem'd, and sorely smit with pain,
While bare foot as she trod the flinty pavement,
Her footsteps all along were mark'd with blood.
Yet silent still she pass'd and unrepining;
Her streaming eyes bent ever on the earth,
Except when in some bitter pang of sorrow,
To Heaven she seem'd in fervent zeal to raise them,
And beg that mercy man denied her here. (II, 174)

Moreover, Jane's ordeal has not ended; for Bellmour tells Shore that "a churlish guard attends upon her steps" to keep anyone from offering her comfort or, indeed, even food and water.

Shore is resolved that, whatever the consequences, he will give her help; and he will do so in his own person: he will no longer play a false role. Bellmour, who thinks such an action will be more upsetting to Jane than Shore might suppose, says to Shore, "Has mercy fix'd her empire there so sure,/ That wrath and vengeance never may return?" (II, 175). And by his question, he obliges Shore to remember and to recount the story of Jane's seduction by Edward, a tale almost as moving as Bellmour's description of her present plight. In Shore's long, almost uninterrupted recital of his love and devotion to her and of the king's triumph, Shore makes the domestic tragedy complete. It is not enough that we are aware of Jane's tragic end; Shore as her husband, and therefore as the representative of family virtue and law, must have his part too.

In this recital of the woeful past, Bellmour serves to remind Shore that Jane's very sweetness had betrayed her; her fatal beauty had caused her fall. Shore, remembering that delicate beauty, knows she cannot long exist "hunted to death, distress'd on every side,/

With no one hand to help." In Shore's speech in answer to
Bellmour, Rowe again shows his ability to engage our pity for the
beautiful sinner-saint figure that Jane represents. Recalling the days
when for her "the merchant spread his silken stores," Shore ends his
speech,

> Can she—
> Intreat for bread, and want the needful rainment,
> To wrap her shiv'ring bosom from the weather?
> When she was mine, no care came ever nigh her.
> I thought the gentlest breeze that wakes the spring
> Too rough to breathe upon her; cheerfulness
> Danc'd all the day before her; and at night
> Soft slumber waited on her downy pillow—
> Now sad and shelterless, perhaps, she lies,
> Where piercing winds blow sharp, and the chill rain
> Drops from some pent-house on her wretched head,
> Drenches her locks, and kills her with the cold.   (II, 177)

When Shore and Bellmour find Jane, her appearance is more
alarming than in Bellmour's description. She has been wandering
about for two days without food or shelter; and she is still barefoot,
she still wears disheveled clothes, and her hair still hangs loose and
unkempt. When Jane realizes Shore's true identity, she faints; and,
when she is revived, she protests in rhetorical, rather than conventional words. Shore will have no set speeches. He says to her quite
simply:

> Why dost thou turn away?—Why tremble thus?
> Why thus indulge thy fears? And in despair,
> Abandon thy distracted soul to horror?
> Cast every black and guilty thought behind thee,
> And let 'em never vex thy quiet more.
> My arms, my heart are open to receive thee,
> To bring thee back to thy forsaken home,
> With tender joy, with fond forgiving love,
> And all the longings of my first desires.   (II, 182)

In this final passage of the play, Rowe turns away from the man-
nered, bombastic speech of the earlier scenes—the usual speeches
of his plays and his theater—and writes in terms of simple, natural
dignity. Shore offers her food, and Jane, taking it, remembers,

> How can you be so good?
> But you were ever thus; I well remember
> With what fond care, what diligence of love,
> You lavish'd out your wealth to buy me pleasures,
> Preventing every wish: have you forgot
> The costly string of pearl you brought me home,
> And tied about my neck?—How could I leave you?   (II, 183)

The pearl, a symbol of purity, has now become for Jane the remembrance of a time of innocence and love. But, as she intently looks at Shore, she realizes that the past is not the present—he has become old, wrinkled, full of sorrow. She has herself caused his grief; and, while she cannot recall the past, she can be sorry about her transgressions. Overcome with her guilt and grief, she faints; and Shore has to seek help to support her. At this moment, the guard arrives, but Jane cannot part with Shore. Before she dies, she must receive from him, as from God Himself, forgiveness and absolution; and Jane, who is very close to death, can only murmur, "Forgive me!—but forgive me!"

Jane's last request to her husband for his forgiveness is that of the saint and the now martyr; and even the great Dr. Samuel Johnson, who did not approve of the pathetic in poetry, was said to have been moved by her words.[8] Into the midst of the solemn final scene, the guards, symbols of the heartless tyranny of Gloucester, now Richard III, intrude; but both Shore and Bellmour, no longer concerned about the dead Jane, care no more about what the "tyrant's will" can do to them.

Rowe's handling of the final scene of the play shows his intention quite clearly: Jane too must pay a penalty for her loss of virtue. She has forsaken her husband, a sin far more culpable than becoming mistress of a nobleman as Alicia has done. Jane must not only repent and refuse to yield to further temptation; she must do public penance but, in the end, even that is not enough. Only through the forgiveness of Shore, her wronged husband, can she achieve sainthood. The tragedy was Jane's; it was a "she-tragedy," a phrase itself taken from the Epilogue of this play and subsequently used to identify Rowe's special contribution to the domestic tragedy that became increasingly popular in the development of eighteenth-century drama. Rowe meant to stir our pity, to move us to make our response to Jane. Beautiful and sweet, she shared with all the other women their weaknesses and their sense of the ultimate tragic irony of fate. When she had repented, denied passion, and clung to virtue, she had not the power or the privilege to direct her own life. The violent intrusion of the guards in the last scene reminds us of the fatal irony of a world controlled by tyranny.

Alicia too is a part of the conclusion. With no one to love her—to care for or about her—she is completely lost. Hastings, like Lothario in *The Fair Penitent*, discards her when he pleases. Hers is in reality a more desolate fate than Jane's—she is offered no means of redemption. And her final madness is the inevitable consequence of the loss of love. Whatever our immediate response to the conclusion of the play, our critical judgment of the whole of it must take into account both of the themes Rowe presented—the theme of love and the theme of loyalty; for each is equally important to family and country.

VII   Jane Shore: *Rowe's Masterpiece*

As we have said, *Jane Shore* was immediately popular upon its initial presentation; it remained so for almost two centuries.[9] Since it was one of the first plays to be advertised with what was apparently an elaborately conducted campaign, and since the play became a stock one in repertory companies throughout England and Ireland (and later in America), the role of Jane Shore and that of Alicia became favored ones for a long line of famous actresses.

In selecting Jane Shore as his protagonist, Rowe again, as in his character of Calista, left himself open to criticism about the suitability of his choice. There were those who found Jane socially unsuitable as well as morally degenerate. Charles Gildon has Truewit in *A New Rehearsal* deny that the play is tragedy even when he describes it as "really a very merry Tragedy, there are but six Men and two Women in it; the two Women are Whores, and three of the Men Villains, one a Cuckold and another a Debocher of young Ladies. . . ." Moreover, Rowe's announced attempt to imitate Shakespeare's style brought skepticism and witty comment from some of his contemporaries.[10]

The play answers all such criticism. Jane herself is the focus of the whole design; and, as the sinner-saint figure, she is more than a merchant's wife favored by the king; she is the epitome of all the frailty of feminine beauty. Like Helen of Troy, hers is the fatal power of great beauty, not the pathetic weakness of the soft, yielding Calista. Moreover, Jane is the focal point of the political themes of the play; for both personal and public themes are combined in her misfortunes. In the final moments when Jane is tenderly united with her husband and becomes no longer the sinner-saint but the redeemed and redeeming angel, the injustice of the world and the tyranny of wickedness are clearly revealed. When Mrs. Oldfield, who created the role, or Mrs. Siddons, who was notable in it, appeared as the forgiving and forgiven saint, it is no wonder that the audience should be moved by Jane's murmured "Forgive me!—but Forgive me!"[11]

Recent criticism of *Jane Shore* has not only recognized it as Rowe's masterpiece but also as the best example of his "she-tragedy." This play demonstrates his skill in turning the focus of tragedy in his theater away from the artificial, contrived plot to the simple story, from the heroic manner to the domestic situation. Moreover, *Jane Shore* contains some of Rowe's best poetry. In the description of Jane's walk through London, in Shore's description of her departure from his household, when, riding with the king in the royal carriage, she sees Shore, and weeps; in the moving recital of her abandonment when she is turned away from Alicia's door and refused food after she has wandered in the streets for three days and nights—in all these places Rowe has turned his skill in writing smooth, flowing, elegant verse to making his poetry the means whereby he moves his audience to pity and to tears.

One critic, writing about *Jane Shore,* has said: "In his masterpiece, *Jane Shore,* Rowe found the type of tragic drama which suited exactly the popular taste of his age and which best represents it to the modern reader. . . . With the production of *Jane Shore,* Rowe's popularity as a tragic poet was unrivaled. . . . he won the sympathy of his audience for the sufferings of his repentent sinner."[12] And another critic has seen the "pleasant simplicity in much of the language."[13] By the short simple speeches in the last scene of the play as Jane is dying and by Shore's simple declarations of love for her in his final speeches, Rowe's poetry is so effective that the audience forgot that one could not starve in an afternoon or that domestic grief would not outweigh public faction. Gloucester's tyranny, Hastings's haughty scorn, and the remembered passing of the dead King Edward are all turned to the farewell speeches of a man and his wife, of her prayer for forgiveness for her infidelity, and of his declaration of love. Both as Rowe's best play and as a memorable one in his theater, *Jane Shore* deserves attention.

CHAPTER 8

Lady Jane Gray:
Rowe's Portrait of a Queen

*L*ADY Jane Gray, Rowe's next play after the success of *Jane Shore*, was performed little more than a year later at Drury Lane on April 20, 1715. The same group of players acted in *Lady Jane Gray* as in *Jane Shore;* and *Lady Jane*, like *Jane Shore*, had an elaborate advertising campaign before its appearance. Books were revived and republished to furnish playgoers with the proper remembrances of Lady Jane Gray's true and tragic history.[1]

One twentieth-century critic says that Rowe in *Lady Jane Gray* "repeated the genre, but not the success of *Jane Shore*";[2] and Gildon, who wrote a whole pamphlet entitled *Remarks on Mr. Rowe's Tragedy of the Lady Jane Gray* (1715), observes that "The whore found more favour with the Town than the Saint."[3] These comments may be regarded as typical of those of one group of critics; but *Lady Jane Gray* has always had its defenders. Like each of Rowe's other tragedies, the production was a success in its first run; and Dibdin remarks that, when it was first performed, it "was then well received, and has often been repeated, with considerable success."[4] Baker in the *Biographia Dramatica* commends it: "On the whole, I think I may venture to pronounce it equal to any, and superior to most, of the dramatic pieces of this admirable author."[5] Rowe himself certainly intended it to be an elegant and polished piece of poetry and of drama; and, if we are to consider it as in the same genre as *Jane Shore*, we must be precise in our discussion of how it fits into the same category, for it is a very different play from *Jane Shore*.

I *Sources and Themes*

Rowe dedicated *Lady Jane Gray* to Caroline of Anspach, the Princess Royal. Rowe could indeed be grateful to George I, the new monarch, and his family; for, in the brief space of eight months after Anne's death on August 1, 1714, Rowe had been appointed Land Surveyor of Customs and in little over a year he was to be made Poet Laureate and Clerk of the Council to the Prince of Wales. It was fitting that he should offer such a dignified review of an earlier, troubled time of British history even though there was no tragic parallel to Lady Jane Gray when the House of Hanover ascended the throne. Anne had, in the last months before her death, steadily refused to discuss the succession; and there were hundreds of rumors in those weeks and months to the effect that she herself was giving aid to a scheme whereby her Tory minister would proclaim James III her successor. In the preface to the printed version of *Lady Jane Gray*, Rowe dates his writing with a reference to "in the beginning of the last summer"; for precisely at that time the fears for the Protestant Succession had been most vigorously revived.

From the very beginning of the play, then, Rowe makes his purpose clear. There is a marked contrast between the two "Janes," for Lady Jane was no sinner-saint—she was, as Rowe says in the opening lines of his Prologue, "A heroine, a martyr, and a queen." Moreover, he would have his audience copy the "beauteous saint," for

> No guilty wish inflam'd her spotless brest:
> The only love that warm'd her blooming youth,
> Was husband, England, liberty, and truth.
> For these she fell; while, with too weak a hand,
> She strove to save a blind ungrateful land.   (II, 193)

Rowe could hardly have been more explicit in making precise the application of the meaning of the play. Lady Jane lost everything for a just cause when the efforts to continue the Protestant Succession upon the death of Edward VI, Henry VIII's only son, had ended in her death and in disaster for her followers. In a later time, the precise time of Rowe's play, a grateful Britain is to be thankful that the House of Hanover has been willing to secure the Protestant Succession that William III made possible. Given the particular situation of the Hanoverian Succession and the remembrance of English history in another much-disputed succession, Rowe had a ready-made dramatic situation upon which to draw.

Moreover, he also had some slight help from Edmund Smith, a friend of his who had been at Christ College, Oxford, who had worked on a play about Lady Jane for some years and who at his death had left his papers to Rowe. Smith had evidently worked on a play designed to be in the pathetic tradition of John Bank's *The Innocent Usurper*, a play prohibited "on account of some mistaken censures and groundless insinuations that it reflected on the government."[6] But Rowe says that, instead of finding in Smith's papers "a whole design regularly drawn out," he found "about two quires of paper written over in odd pieces, blotted, interlined, and confused" (II, 192). The play is, therefore, Rowe's own handiwork, and it in no way made "groundless insinuations that reflected on the government." It exhibits even more than *Jane Shore* Rowe's two interests: the pathos of the beautiful, tragic woman—the "she-tragedy"—and his constant support of liberty and order in government.

II *The Dramatic Action*

The dramatic action of the play is slight, and there are few complications. Indeed, the historical facts of the story of Lady Jane Gray alone furnished all the incidents Rowe needed. Lady Jane was the daughter of the Duke and Duchess of Suffolk and the great-granddaughter of Henry VII. Her marriage to Lord Guildford Dudley, the youngest son of the Duke of Northumberland, was arranged to promote the older Northumberland's political intrigues. At first, Northumberland's plans suceeded; for, persuading the dying King Edward VI, Henry VIII's only son, to approve his schemes, he had Protestant Lady Jane declared queen instead of Catholic Princess Mary, Henry VIII's elder daughter. Nine days later, the council reversed its approval; and Lady Jane and her husband Lord Dudley were seized and committed to the Tower of London. Through no deed or word of her own, she became a pawn in the troubled line of succession after the close of Henry VIII's reign and also a part of the conflict between the church and the state which Henry VIII had begun when he broke with Rome and declared himself the head of the Church of England as well as the king of England. Both Lady

Jane and her husband were executed for treason, and the Princess Mary became queen.

Taking this material, Rowe modified it for his own purposes. He added the theme of friendship between Guilford and Pembroke, the two rivals for Jane's hand; he suggested that Edward had designated Jane to be queen on his death, asking her to be good to England and keep the faith—the Protestant faith in which they had both been bred; he removes the burden of guilt for Lady Jane's death from Queen Mary to her priest, Gardiner; and he heightens the dramatic tension of the last part of the play by suggesting that Lady Jane and her husband were offered a reprieve if they would recant and swear allegiance to Rome. *Lady Jane Gray* was, as Rowe said, of his own design and of his own execution throughout.

Moreover, Rowe achieves a kind of epic unity in this drama that he does not match in any other play. Perhaps he loses some of the domestic pathos of *Jane Shore* by centering attention on Lady Jane, but by this concentration on his martyred queen he gains a kind of classic simplicity. We are not distracted by a powerful figure like Gloucester who must impose his own plot, or by passionate ones like Alicia or Hastings who are rivals for the attention that Jane herself should have in the play. *Lady Jane Gray* is a series of vignettes that reveal Lady Jane's tragic story, a story wholly involved with church and state.

The basic plot of the play—Rowe's version of the facts of history—may quickly be told. Edward upon his deathbed urged Lady Jane "do thou be good to England," and he prayed earnestly to God to "Protect this land from bloody men and idols/ Save my poor people from the yoke of *Rome.*" Lady Jane then, because of her loyalty and devotion to her cousin, is willing to marry Guilford, the son and heir of the Duke of Northumberland, even though her interest is in executing her dying king's wish far more than in gaining a husband.

The elder members of the families involved, the Duke and Duchess of Suffolk as well as the Duke of Northumberland, unlike Lady Jane, are more interested in promoting themselves than in protecting England and the church. Lady Jane's grief over Edward's death and her zeal to follow his commands, aside from the contrivances of Suffolk and Northumberland, bring about her marriage. The success of their scheme is of brief duration, for the political conflict among the great nobles is such that Lady Jane's right to the throne is immediately challenged. In the end, their attempt to take the throne completely thwarted, she and her husband are captured and imprisoned in the Tower.

In addition to the main plot of the play, there is the conflict of friendship and love between Guilford and the Earl of Pembroke, who had also sought the hand of Lady Jane and who is furious when, without his knowledge, she is married by her parents to Guilford. In this political conflict in the early part of the play, Pembroke is captured and imprisoned by the faction led by Guilford. While in the Tower, Pembroke becomes acquainted with Gardiner, Roman Bishop of Winchester, who is also held captive by the faction. From their acquaintance, the subsequent action of this part of the play develops. For a brief time the supporters of Lady Jane—Guilford, now her husband; her father Suffolk; and Northumberland—seize power and control London.

Gardiner, Bishop of Winchester, who is a powerful figure both in the Roman Catholic Church and in the political group opposed to Lady Jane and her followers, predicts to Pembroke that "holy vengeance" will not "loiter long," that "The nobles of the land, and swarming populace/ Gather, and list beneath her Princess Mary royal ensigns" (II, 224). In the brief time before his prediction becomes fact, when Gardiner is sent to be closely confined, Guilford has the opportunity to release Pembroke. Shortly thereafter when, in a quick reversal of fortune, Lady Jane and Guilford, losing their battle to retain the throne, are imprisoned, Pembroke returns the mercy Guilford gave him. Pembroke as messenger from Queen Mary, now firmly placed upon the throne, offers both Lady Jane and Guilford their freedom; but even as he does so his speech is interrupted by the priest Gardiner, who qualifies the pardon by saying that Lady Jane and Guilford must swear allegiance to Rome as well as to the queen. When both refuse to do so, the action of the play ends with the execution, first of Guilford and then of Lady Jane herself.

III   *The Interwoven Fabric of Loyalties*

However slight the action of *Lady Jane Gray* may be, it is sufficient to carry the themes that make up the major interest of the play. These themes, established in the exposition of the first act, are woven together in such a way that the play becomes a play of themes, not of character or plot, As the play opens, Edward is already beyond human aid; the Duke of Northumberland and the Duke of Suffolk converse with their friend Sir John Gates about the church and the throne. Suffolk is already concerned for his country as he says, "Religion melts in ev'ry holy eye,/ All comfortless, and forlorn/ She sits on earth, and weeps upon her cross" (II, 195). The years have been short ones since the English church "late from heaps of *Gothic* ruins rose/ In her first native simple majesty" and Suffolk very much fears that "again old Rome/ Shall spread her banners; and her Monkish host, Pride, ignorance, and rapine shall return" (II, 195). But Suffolk's speech characterizing Mary is not personal; it reminds Rowe's audience of the traits traditionally assigned to Rome.

Northumberland, Suffolk, and Gates pledge to resist "proud presuming Romish Priests," and never to "Bow down before the holy purple tyrants," of Rome. Such declarations are not enough; political action must be swift and vigorous. The scheme to place Lady Jane upon the throne must have wide support, and the aid of the Earl of Pembroke is sought. Pembroke and Guilford are friends; Pembroke calls Guilford "The noblest youth our England has." Their rivalry for Lady Jane has not separated them. And thus their friendship, introduced early in the first act establishes another major theme of the play.

Rowe has made their relationship as exactly Elizabethan as would fit his play. They are noble youths, full of courage, bound by the courtly code of ethics, and skilled in courtesy. Pembroke is filled with passionate pride; Guilford, with ideal loyalty. Their responses to each other and to Lady Jane delineate two Renaissance court portraits. When Guilford first meets Lady Jane, all is fortune and fate; and they talk as if they stood in the woods of Sidney's *Arcadia*, unaware of anyone or anything except their own emotional responses. Pembroke cannot bear defeat; Guilford, the more even-tempered of the two men, is also the more generous. In their first discussion of their rivalry, Pembroke concludes that they must remember "Our friendship and our honour" and that they should contend "as friends and brave men ought,/ With openness and justice to each other." Guilford, left alone, speaks:

> How cross the ways of life lie! While we think
> We travel on direct in one high road,

And have our journey's end oppos'd in view,
A thousand thwarting paths break in upon us,
To puzzle and perplex our wand'ring steps.
Love, friendship, hatred, in their turns mislead us,
And ev'ry passion has its separate interest.
Where is that piercing foresight can unfold
Where all this mazy error will have end,
And tell the doom reserv'd for me and Pembroke!
There is but one end certain, that is—Death:
Yet ev'n that certainty is still uncertain.
For of these several tracks which lie before us,
We know that one leads certainly to death,
But know not which that one is. 'Tis in vain,
This blind divining; let me think no more on't: (II, 200–201)

But his musing is interrupted by Lady Jane herself. Guilford addresses her in the same mood of courtly speech as he has used with Pembroke. He compares her to the moon, the "silver regent of the night," and he would have her "sacred beams" help "dispel our horrors/ And make us less lament the setting sun" (II, 201). Lady Jane is in a somber mood—she has just left the dying King Edward, and she is full of fear for the fate of England. But Guilford forgets the dangers to his country; he gazes into Lady Jane's eyes and wonders "how excelling nature/ Can give each day new patterns of her skill,/ And yet at once surpass 'em" (II, 202). She will have none of his fair speech; she would rather hear "the raven's note"; it strikes her ear more sweetly. She ends the scene and, in fact, the first act with a somber speech suited to her mood of despair. The Elizabethan and Renaissance qualities of the early scenes in the act have made way for the seventeenth-century dirge of death.

IV   *The Dark Thread of Death*

It is fitting that the play as Rowe conceived it should be turned frequently to the theme of death. The historical episode of Lady Jane Gray was itself remembered largely in the context of death and the church, for these two topics were as current for Rowe's audience as politics and economics are constant themes for the twentieth century. The significant point in *Lady Jane Gray* is the way in which the two themes are handled. In this play, unlike the earlier ones, we have none of the shrill exaggeration of the charnel scene in *The Fair*

Penitent or of the bombastic declarations of *The Ambitious Step-Mother* or, for that matter, the rather platitudinous attitudes found in *Ulysses* and in *The Royal Convert*. It was a fact that Lady Jane Gray had briefly been a queen—made so by her family and their supporters—to insure a Protestant succession. It was natural for her to examine her position, purge her soul, and meditate upon death. Given the vogue for the "grave-yard" literature of the early eighteenth century, Rowe's handling of the theme in *Lady Jane Gray* is dignified, sane, and proper; it befits the kind of matter a Poet Laureate would compose; and it is suitable for dedication to a royal princess.

One of Rowe's real problems in the play is to introduce and develop the theme of love in such a way that it does not detract from the serious contemplation of death and the dangers to England and the church attendant upon the loss of the young king. Lady Jane is young and beautiful, and both Guilford and Pembroke are passionately in love with her, but her response to the palpable hand of death upon her beloved Edward and her almost immediate personal encounter with it allows little time—or place—for a consideration of love or joy with anyone under any circumstances.

In the first scene of the second act, all the principals—Northumberland, Suffolk, Guilford, the Duchess of Suffolk—attempt to reconcile the two topics, death and love. They understand clearly that they must unite the two families—that Lady Jane, the daughter of the Duke of Suffolk, and Guilford, the son of the Duke of Northumberland, must be married to each other to insure the unity of the two families. They also realize that, since the young Edward VI is dying, their hope of having Jane become his queen must be immediately forgotten. They must turn from his death to Jane's future, and they must act quickly. This scene is an especially important one as each of the principal characters in it adds to the delicate reconciliation. Northumberland sets the tone of the whole scene when he says:

> Doubt not any thing;
> Nor hold the hour unlucky, that good Heav'n,
> Who softens the corrections of his hand,
> And mixes still a comfort with afflictions,
> Has giv'n to-day a blessing in our children,
> To wipe away our tears for dying Edward.   (II, 203)

Guilford is gracious and proper; the Duchess of Suffolk is equally so. Northumberland, speaking to them both, describes Lady Jane as "All desolate and drown'd in flowing tears, By Edward's bed the pious princess sits" (II, 204); when Lady Suffolk replies to this remark, the audience is hardly aware that she is establishing the legal basis for their attempt to set aside Princess Mary and to make Lady Jane the queen.

Rowe's handling of this problem of reconciling death and love is delicate and sure. Guilford as Lady Jane's future husband must bring together fate, love, death—for these are all interwoven in the larger themes of loyalty to church and state. He would have her "give one interval to joy," and, when she agrees, his speech is tender and considerate. In a subtle way, he uses the idea of death to plead his own cause as he says,

> . . . our noble parents had decreed,
> And urg'd high reasons which import the state,
> This night to give thee to my faithful arms,
> . . . .
> Yet if thou art resolv'd to cross my fate,
> If this my utmost wish shall give thee pain,
> Now rather let the stroke of death fall on me,
> And stretch me out a lifeless corse before thee:
> Let me be swept away with things forgotten,
> Be huddled up in some obscure blind grave,
> Ere thou should'st say my love has made thee wretched,
> Or drop one single tear for Guilford's sake.   (II, 206)

Lady Jane's response, "Alas! I have too much of death already," is simple and natural; but it cannot make proper a scene that includes the monstrous and macabre in its unnatural juxtaposition of life and death. As if seeing the inappropriateness of their conversation, Guilford offers to leave the marriage unconsummated until, as he says, "at thy pleasure" she may portion out the blessings. He will go away; he will leave her alone, but Lady Jane would have a companion in her sorrow. Offering him her hand, she says, "Here then I take thee to my heart forever,/ The dear companion of my future days;/ Whatever Providence allots for each,/ Be that the common portion of us both" (II, 207). Their concluding dialogue in this scene is a duet of poetry. Indeed, the whole of the scene might have been written for the opera—it begins in a recitative that quickly sets the

future action of the play and then becomes a long lyric composition
of love and melancholy sorrow, not yet tragic, but with the promise
of becoming so. To Guilford, Lady Jane says,

> Trust our fate
> To him whose gracious wisdom guides our ways,
> And makes what we think evil turn to good.
> . . . .
> My private loss no longer will I mourn,
> . . . .
> But oh? when I revolve what ruins wait
> Our sinking altars, and the falling state:
> . . . .
> My whole heart for wretched England bleeds.   (II, 208)

And after she leaves, Guilford, reviewing their situation, finds little
prospect of joy. Even as he says he could "muse away an age in
deepest melancholy," Pembroke appears and begins to speak of
Edward's death; but he is immediately aware that something of
great consequence has occurred since he last saw Guilford. Guilford
tries to prepare him for the news; but Pembroke, impatient and
hasty, partly guesses it and is so furious about the marriage that,
although Guilford would temper the blow, Pembroke calls him a
traitor, threatens his life, and denounces their friendship.

Again Rowe has written a scene of passion in which the uncontrolled fury of Pembroke is matched by the reason of Guilford—
reason that is the warm, genuine support of the ties of friendship.
This confrontation between Pembroke and Guilford is a more be-
lieveable, if less dramatic, scene than the ones between Hastings
and Jane Shore or between Alicia and Hastings in *Jane Shore*. Refusing to fight, Guilford will not profane the sacred grounds of the court
"with brawls and outrage"; but Pembroke, who will listen to nothing, declares:" . . . when we meet again, may swift destruction/ Rid
me of thee, or rid me of myself" (II, 212). Whereupon Pembroke
leaves; and Guilford, having lost a friend and made an enemy—all
for love—is left alone.

V   *The Themes of Church and State*

By Act III the situation of the play has been so well established
that the themes of church and state may be seriously considered in

the context of the action and in the plans made by Northumberland,
the Suffolks, and Guilford. Gardiner, the priest of Rome, has long
been held prisoner; and Pembroke has just arrived in the Tower,
placed there by Northumberland, now head of the Protestant faction. Gardiner's first speech shows his cunning awareness of both
the political situation and Pembroke's personal disappointment.
Warning Pembroke "to be master of yourself," he reveals that he
has learned "yester ev'ning late,/ In spite of all the grief for Edward's death,/ Your friends were married" (II, 213). Pembroke, still
totally unreconciled to his situation, gives, nevertheless, a beautiful
encomium to Lady Jane:

> The virtues came,
> Sorted in gentle fellowship, to crown her,
> As if they meant to mend each other's work,
> Candor with goodness, fortitude with sweetness,
> Strict piety, and love of truth, with learning,
> More than the schools of Athens ever knew,
> Or her own *Plato* taught. A wonder!   (II, 214)

And while Gardiner agrees, he has still more information; perhaps
Pembroke may yet possess the Lady Jane. If the rebellion mounted
by Northumberland, Suffolk, and Guilford is thwarted, perhaps
Guilford will be slain in the conflict. Pembroke cannot believe in
such an eventuality; but he agrees, for his "sweet revenge," to aid in
Gardiner's plan to support the Princess Mary.

The scene between Pembroke and Gardiner in the Tower is followed by one between the new-made bride and groom who also talk
of love and loyalty. Still lamenting Edward's loss, still concerned
with death, Lady Jane feels somehow that grief awaits them at every
turn. It is only at this point that she realizes the plan that her
husband and her father have made. In amazement, she cannot believe Guilford. Her mother, the Duchess of Suffolk, entering, commands her,

> No more complain, indulge thy tears no more,
> Thy pious grief has giv'n the grave its due;
> Let thy heart kindle with the highest hopes;
> Expand thy bosom, let thy soul enlarg'd
> Make room to entertain the coming glory;
> For majesty and purple greatness court thee;

> Homage and low subjection wait: A crown,
> That makes the princes of the earth like gods
> A crown, my daughter, *England's* crown attends
> To bind thy brows with its imperial wreath, . . .   (II, 217)

The whole vast scheme is now fully revealed to Lady Jane; but, before she fully comprehends her position, the lords from the Council enter to hail her as queen of England. They kneel to her in spite of her protestations. When she turns to Guilford and asks him, "Come to my aid, and help to bear this burthen/ Oh! save me from this sorrow, this misfortune,/ Which in the shape of gorgeous greatness comes/ To crown, and make a wretch of me forever" (II, 219), he, like the other lords, pledges his sword to her support.

Again the action of the play is suspended and each person speaks in turn of man, of his place in the universal scheme of God, of his duties to his own society, and finally of his relationship to his rulers—his king upon this earth and his supreme ruler, God. All the sentiments of the speeches are commonplaces of eighteenth-century thought, but they gain added interest as such for the critic who sees them interwoven into the dramatic fabric of Rowe's play. They gain, moreover, as the critic realizes that Rowe has united the climax of the action and the complexities of the interwoven themes of the play. Church, state, and private destinies are united.

Lady Jane herself sees the responsibilities of the throne, "to watch, to toil, to take a sacred charge,/ To bend each day before high Heav'n" (II, 220). Her mother offers tribute to the English monarchs of the past "who liv'd not for themselves." Suffolk paints a lurid and dramatic picture of what will happen if Rome's Mary should be triumphant. Towns and churches will burn, "Our youth on racks shall stretch their crackling bones," and the land will be filled with "a continu'd peal/ Of lamentations, groans, and shrieks" (II, 221). Guilford makes his plea for the liberty of his land and his people. In the final line of the scene—the final line of Act III—Lady Jane, though she knows her doom is inevitable, agrees to do what she can "To save this land from tyranny and *Rome*" (II, 224).

But Lady Jane's acceptance does not close the discussion; the views of the others must be presented. The beginning of the fourth act continues the scene of the preceding one, but the actors are changed. Instead of Lady Jane Gray and her sponsors, Pembroke and Gardiner discuss their view of the situation. Gardiner characterizes Northumberland as "that traitor Duke," and he prays to "holy Becket, the protector/ The Champion, and the martyr of our Church" to appear "And cover foul rebellion with confusion." Pembroke has seen Northumberland, armed for battle, issue from the city gate and pass in eerie silence through "a staring ghastly-looking crowd/ Unhail'd unbless'd, . . ." (II, 224). Gardiner is certain that Mary and her cause will prevail; but, before the triumph of the Catholic Queen Mary and her Roman priest, Gardiner, the fate of Lady Jane and her Guilford must be played out; and the themes of friendship and love must be finished.

At this point in the action, Guilford comes to rescue Pembroke from his confinement in the Tower. Pembroke is caught between his sworn allegiance to Mary and Guilford's generous action; and where his loyalty lies becomes a nice question—one that again reveals Rowe's use of the traditions of the Renaissance view of such a friendship, a tradition that sees friendship as permanent and binding as love between father and son or between man and woman. Persuaded that Guilford speaks as friend, Pembroke agrees to take his sword and escape; and he declares to Guilford as he does so that all there is of good or excellence in man may be found in the bond of friendship. With this evidence of friendship, the theme is complete; but, when Pembroke offers Guilford and Lady Jane their freedom later in the closing drama of their doom, his friendship is not enough to save them. Pembroke's loyalty to Mary cancelled the loyalty of friendship. The Roman Catholic Church offers mercy only to those who will accept its tenets—the mercy of friendship is not enough to pardon Guilford and Lady Jane.

VI *Lady Jane as Saint and Martyr*

In developing Lady Jane as a saint and as a martyr, Rowe has simply extended the traditional virtues of the historical Lady Jane. In Act IV, he shows her reading Plato's *Phaedo.* When Guilford tells her that their cause is lost, she reminds him that now is the time "to bid our souls look out." And as saint and martyr, she must be sacrificed without guilt. Perhaps her very guiltlessness, required to complete Rowe's scheme, makes us admire her but not love her.

In the end, their doom comes quickly; Northumberland is taken prisoner, charged with treason; Mary, hailed queen; the Tower taken by her supporters; and Gardiner released. Lady Jane's premonitions begin to be reality. For her, "The gaudy masque, tedious, and nothing meaning,/ Is vanish'd all at once," and she kneels in "humble adoration of that mercy" that has saved her from "the vast unequal task." In the last moments before they are parted, Guilford and Lady Jane speak together. Again, as in the earlier parts of the play, they converse in dialogue that is a duet; for each extends and harmonizes the thoughts of the other. And again there is the recital of love and death.

This scene, however, is very much in the manner of pathos— indeed, of sentimentality. Guilford marvels at Lady Jane's cool courage as she faces certain death; she who has wept before has now no tears. Her last two speeches return to the more universal senti- ments of Rowe and his audience. She speaks of the "great Creator's never-ceasing hand" and of the even pattern of the cycle of lif₃ and death in God's great Providence:

> 'Tis true, by those dark paths our journey leads,
> And through the vale of death we pass to life,
> But what is there in death to blast our hopes?
> Behold the universal works of nature,
> Where life still springs from death. To us the sun
> Dies every night, and ev'ry morn revives:
> The flow'rs, which Winter's icy hand destroy'd,
> Lift their fair heads, and live again in Spring,
> Mark with what hopes, upon the furrow'd plain,
> The careful ploughman casts the pregnant grain;
> There hid, as in a grave a-while it lies,
> Till the revolving season bids it rise;
> Till nature's genial pow'rs command a birth;
> And potent, call it from the teeming earth;
> Then large increase the buried treasures yield,
> And with full harvest crown the plenteous field.   (II, 236)

Rowe's invention of the incident of Pembroke's appearance in the final act is a nice touch that serves to add intensity to the pathos of Lady Jane and Guilford's fate. Pemproke has a conditional pardon from Queen Mary, and it is his means of repaying Guilford's mag- nanimity to him when his life, like Guilford's now, was in danger. His speech on mercy, with its reference to Mary, is a good one:

> 'Tis mercy! mercy,
> The mark of Heav'n impress'd on human kind;
> Mercy, that glads the world, deals joy around;

> Mercy, that smooths the dreadful brow of power,
> And makes dominion light; mercy, that saves,
> Binds up the broken heart, and heals despair.   (II, 238)

But Gardiner will have no mercy extended to the two royal prisoners. He gives the justification for his views when he defends his judgment that they must be executed for Queen Mary's sake and, even more, for the position of the Roman Catholic Church. Pembroke argues that the church—the Church Universal—offers love and mercy for all when he says "Is not the sacred purpose of our faith/ Peace and good-will to man? The hallow'd hand,/ Ordain'd to bless, should know no stain of blood" (II, 239–40). Again, as in earlier discussions of the topical matters of the day, this scene must have held interest for Rowe and his audience, however dated it may seem to us.

Having shown Lady Jane as blameless, Rowe must now show her to be a saint. The last two scenes in the play are "set" scenes—pictures without action. The directions for the first of these are significant: "The SCENE draws, and discovers the Lady Jane kneeling, as at her devotion; a light, and a book plac'd on a table before her" (II, 240). In *Jane Shore*, there is no such tableau; indeed, Jane's procession of public penance is related by Bellmour; and, effective as his recital is, it cannot be a substitute for the experience of personal observation. Jane, who kneels in prayer, is dressed in her black robes and has the open Bible before her—quite an effective bit of staging. This portrayal is reinforced by her maid's report that Jane had risen before midnight, dressed herself, knelt, and "fix'd her eye upon the sacred page before her,/ Or lifted with her rising hopes to Heav'n." The maid's report is followed by Guilford's even more impassioned words as he sees her already as a saint and as a martyr.

Moreover, as Lady Jane comes forward toward Guilford and the maid, she makes a difficult transition to the real world, saying to Guilford, "Wherefore dost thou come . . . I meant to part without another pang,/ And lay my weary head down full of peace" (II, 241). Rowe's task of reintroducing and keeping alive the love elements of this scene is a difficult one. Guilford himself must carry most of the sentiments, for Lady Jane is so completely the saint, has already become so absorbed with death, that she has little to say of love.

Pembroke arrives dramatically at this point, and the action of the

plot is revived for a brief moment. Pembroke offers his pardons, and
he and Guilford are reunited. Both Lady Jane and Guilford are
saints; he prays that the new queen be blest, for she has spared his
wife. Gardiner has had his will, for he returns from the queen to
demand of Lady Jane and Guilford that they "Do instantly re-
nounce, abjure your heresy,/ And yield obedience to the See of
Rome" (II, 243). Pembroke refuses to believe the queen to be so
merciless, and both Lady Jane and Guilford refuse to disavow their
faith. When Gardiner says "Death, or the mass, attend you," Guilford simply says, "'Tis determin'd:/ Lead to the scaffold." Guilford is
led off by the guards.

Again in a set scene Rowe shows, a scaffold hung with black, with
executioners and guards silently waiting. In the face of her
executioners Gardiner once more asks Lady Jane to "repent, be
wise, and save your precious life," but she again refuses in a speech
that is topical and significant:

> . . . Thou, gracious Heav'n,
> Hear and defend at length thy suffering people;
> Raise up a monarch of the royal blood,
> Brave, pious, equitable, wise and good:
> In thy due season let the hero come,
> To save the altars from the rage of Rome:
> Long let him reign, to bless the rescu'd land,
> And deal out justice with a righteous hand,
> And when he fails, oh! may he leave a son,
> With equal virtues to adorn his throne;
> To latest times the blessing to convey
> And guard that faith for which I die to-day.   (II, 246)

Lady Jane climbs the scaffold, and the scene closes. Two characters
remain on the stage, Gardiner and Pembroke; and Rowe's final
message is Pembroke's conclusion to Gardiner—a conclusion
worthy of the eighteenth-century compromise:

> . . . Who gave thee to explore
> The secret purposes of Heaven, or taught thee
> To set a bound to mercy unconfin'd?
> But know, thou proud, perversely-judging *Winchester*,
> Howev'r you hard, imperious censures doom,
> And portion out our lot in worlds to come,

Those, who, with honest hearts, pursue the right,
And follow faithfully truth's sacred light,
Tho' suff'ring here, shall from their sorrows cease,
Rest with the saints, and dwell in endless peace.   (II, 247)

VII   *The Topical Significance of the Themes*

By late April, 1715, when the actors first discussed the views of
the church and the government set forth in the play before a fash-
ionable London audience, George I was firmly settled as the
monarch. The accomplishment of the peaceful Hanoverian succession must be attributed to a compromise combination of Whigs and
Tories, Dissenter and High Church clergy, combined in a somewhat
uncomfortable alliance of temporary friendship. For, in the previous
year, during the last weeks of Parliament, perhaps just at the time
Rowe began work on his play, a great fight had occurred between
Whigs and Tories; and it centered this time around the Schism Bill
that was designed to close the academies and schools of the Noncon-
formists. The High Church clergy had for years advocated such a
measure, but the Schism Bill itself was political, a measure by the
Tories to curtail the Whigs and the support they received from the
Dissenters.

And, in a larger context, all these concerns were actually aimed at
the continuing battle about the Protestant succession. Many of the
high court officials continued to keep in contact with James III, the
Catholic Pretender. Even the Duke of Marlborough, it was said,
played a double game; indeed, he had probably done so for several
years. In the spring and summer of 1714, there were new rumors
that the Protestant Succession of the Hanoverians was in danger;
there were those who believed that Queen Anne herself secretly
intended to ensure the accession of her half-brother, James III. In
March, 1714, Steele was expelled from Parliament for his pamphlet
The Crisis; and Defoe was again in trouble for a series of pamphlets
he had written under the sponsorship of high officials in Parliament.
All during this time, Anne refused to be bullied into inviting Prince
George or his mother, the Electress Sophia, to come to England to
see their inheritance for themselves.

With Jacobite hopes at the highest point in years, the Schism Act
was passed by a great majority and was to be put into effect on the
first of August. By then, however, the queen was dead, and so was
any hope of the reality of the Schism Act. The Dissenters saw clearly

the remarkable providence of God in the salvation of their schools and academies. In the months of May, June, and July, the quarrels in Parliament to control Queen Anne and the government grew so furious that, ill as she was in these months, Anne rallied once more and reversed the Tory victory relative to the Schism Act. Again, as she had done before, she appointed moderates to the highest places in her government and defeated once again the Tories, who were in sympathy with the Jacobites and the Roman Catholic Church that continued to be the faith of the Pretender, Anne's half-brother James III. Long suffering from the gout, she was not helped by the ministrations of her physicians; and, as the report put it, the gout "translated itself upon the Brain." Many key figures in the Tory party aligned themselves with the moderate Whig Lords; and on July 31 at six o'clock, upon the death of Queen Anne, George I was proclaimed king.[7]

With our knowledge of these political complications in the summer of 1714 we are tempted to speculate about how Rowe composed and adapted the political "lessons" of his play. The historical Lady Jane Gray had been executed because she had been a part of the rebellion against the clear succession of Mary, who by any standard was more nearly in line to the throne than Lady Jane was. Mary was the daughter of Henry VIII; Lady Jane was Mary's cousin—like Mary, the granddaughter of Henry VII. Rowe was always careful in his "lessons" about the succession. He had certainly been precise and direct in discussing both church and state in *The Royal Convert*, and the theme of the succession in *Jane Shore*, while it is only a minor part of the play, is, nevertheless, spoken directly in support of the proper succession of Edward VI's sons. Given then the historical situation and the immediate series of events of the summer of 1714, Rowe must have given a good deal of thought to his focus of themes between church and state.

Viewed in one way, the whole play makes a very strong case for the church and little is said about the problems of the succession. The scene between Gardiner and Pembroke in the early part of the last act is an interesting one for the comments made about the succession. There is much truth in what Gardiner says; and, except for his insistence upon his Roman Catholic faith, he could hardly be disputed since the Princess Mary was more directly in the line of the succession than was Lady Jane. But, when we review the themes of Rowe's play, we become aware of the skill with which he juxtaposed state and church and wove these civil and religious themes together with the personal themes of love and friendship. Pembroke and Queen Mary offered mercy to Lady Jane and Guilford, but Gardiner argues that mercy before treason cannot prevail. There is obviously truth on both sides; and in the spring of 1715 when *Lady Jane Gray* was produced and published there was already a feeling of accommodation within the government and the church.

Once established, the Hanoverians fought for their own rights; and George I, recognizing the need to achieve stability in the government as quickly as possible, brought about a compromise, not only between the political factions of Whigs and Tories, but within the Church of England, especially between the High Church Tories and the Dissenters. From 1715 onward, the church became increasingly latitudinarian in its practice if not by law. Moreover, after 1715, with George I firmly on the throne, the specific problem of the succession was solved; and English political life became centered more and more around economic problems. While the question of the Jacobites continued to trouble the country until the rebellion of 1745, the abortive attempt to place "Bonnie Prince Charlie," the last of the Stuart Pretenders, on the throne of the United Kingdom, the answer to who should occupy the throne was never so ambiguous as it had been in the last years of Queen Anne's reign. By 1745, the attempt to place a Stuart on the throne was clearly an act of rebellion.

Rowe's epilogue to the play repeats his compliments to the Princess Royal and ends with his didactic purpose plainly spelled out:

> Your gratitude with ease may be express'd;
> Strive but to be, what she would make you, bless'd.
> Let not vile faction vex the vulgar ear
> With fond surmise, and false affected fear:
> Confirm but to yourselves the given good;
> 'Tis all she asks, for all she has bestow'd.
> Such was our great example shown to-day,
> And with such thanks our authour's pains repay.
> If from these scenes, to guard your faith you learn,
> If for your laws you show a just concern;
> If you are taught to dread a Popish reign,
> Our beauteous patriot has not died in vain.   (II, 248)

Some of the peculiarly eighteenth-century characteristics of the play have been dismissed as flaws by recent critics. Sutherland, who calls it "dull," asserts that it "is the most tedious and dispiriting of all Rowe's plays."⁸ But earlier critics found many "beauties" in it, and one critic singled out as especially fine the quarrel and reconciliation between Lord Guilford and Lord Pembroke, as well as the scene just before Lady Jane mounts the scaffold which, he found, "has abundance of *pathos* in it."⁹

A Prologue to *Lady Jane Gray* "Sent by an unknown Hand" noted especially Lady Jane's composure before her changing fate. She had "A mind unchang'd, superior to a crown," and she bravely defied "the angry tyrant's frown." "Rowe," the "unknown Hand" said, "draws not beauty's heav'nly smile," but "A nobler passion . . . Then youthful raptures, or the joys of love."¹⁰ Rowe undoubtedly conceived of Lady Jane's character in just such a way. The theme of love could not be omitted, however, and his handling of it under the circumstances is at least adequate for his audience if not pleasing to our more realistic taste.

Lady Jane Gray was Rowe's last play. Along with *The Fair Penitent* and *Jane Shore*, it exemplifies the "she-tragedy" that Rowe promoted. He was not the first to explore the pathos of the beautiful woman in adversity and certainly not the only one in his time. Thomas Heywood's *A Woman Killed with Kindness* evokes quite as much pity as *Jane Shore*; Thomas Otway's *The Orphan*, as *Lady Jane Gray*. Like Calista, Belvederia in Otway's *Venice Preserved* is an ambiguous figure, a woman not wholly good—certainly not wholly bad. In fact, all three of Rowe's "she-tragedies" share the interests of other plays familiar to his audience; but the combinations he made in them; the three principal characters he created—Calista, Jane Shore, and Lady Jane Gray; and his sense of the elegance in drama—the formal speech, music, the set scene—that was the vogue of his own first two decades of the eighteenth century—these characteristics make his plays important beyond any single unique contribution he might have made to the history of the drama. In this context, Lady Jane Gray is the ideal; she had, or was given, all the worthwhile things of this world—beauty, love, power. But, faced with death because of her loyalty to church and country, she made the right choices and assumed the proper eighteenth-century attitudes and sentiments. At a time when the stage was frequently a showcase for topical sentiments and even more frequently a medium for sentimental emotional reactions, *Lady Jane Gray* not surprisingly remained a stock play.

CHAPTER 9

Rowe's Non-Dramatic Work

IN 1715, upon the death of Nahum Tate, Rowe was made Poet
Laureate. In this same year he married again; his second wife was
Anne Devenish; their daughter, Charlotte, was born in 1718, probably in May. In the winter of 1718 Rowe became ill; and his sickness
was widely reported. On November 8, *The Weekly Journal or
British Gazeteer* announced that he lay "so dangerously ill at his
House in Covent Garden that his life is despaired of." Upon his
death on December 6, notices appeared in all the daily and weekly
periodicals. Dr. Welwood, who attended him in his last illness,
wrote:

When he had just got to be easy in his Fortune, and was in a fair way to
make it better, Death swept him away, and in him depriv'd the World of
one of the best Men, as well as one of the best Genius's of the Age. He dy'd
like a *Christian* and a Philosopher, in Charity with all Mankind, and with an
absolute Resignation to the Will of God. He kept up his good Humour to
the last, and took leave of his wife and Friends, immediately before his last
Agony, with the same Tranquility of Mind, and the same indifference for
Life, as tho' he had been upon taking but a short Journey.[1]

Rowe was buried in Westminster Abbey next to Chaucer's monument. Rowe's own monument in the Abbey has had a curious history. His widow, Anne, requested Alexander Pope to write an
epitaph for the tomb she planned for her husband; but, before her
plans were complete, Pope published the verse.[2] In its original
form, it read:

> Thy relics, Rowe, to this fair urn we trust,
> And sacred, place by Dryden's awful dust:
> Beneath a rude and nameless stone he lies,
> To which thy tomb shall guide inquiring eyes.

> Peace to thy gentle shade, and endless rest!
> Blest in thy genius, in thy love, too, blest!
> One grateful woman to thy fame supplies,
> What a whole thankless land to his denies.

The comments about Dryden were effective, for the Duke of Buckingham took the hint and erected a monument to him. The final version of the verse on Rowe's tablet was extended and made a more fitting tribute to him than Pope's first eight lines had been, but it is not certain that Pope was altogether responsible for it.[3] In recent years Rowe's monument has been shifted to uncover an ancient wall painting.

I *Rowe's Translation of Lucan*

Rowe's translation of Lucan's *Pharsalia* was published some three months after his death in 1719. Dedicated to the king by Rowe's widow, this work appeared in two versions—as a handsome special folio subscribed to by such people as the Earl of Halifax and the Duchess of Marlborough, and as an octavo for the general public. Welwood has said of this widely acclaimed work that ". . . perhaps his best Poem is this his Translation of *Lucan*, which he just lived to finish."[4]

Considering Rowe's interest in both drama and politics, he could not have selected a more suitable poet to translate. Marcus Annaeus Lucan, the nephew of Seneca, had written, during Nero's reign, of the civil wars between Caesar and Pompey. In writing about Lucan and his *Pharsalia*, one of the Roman's recent translators has observed that "it consists of carefully chosen, cunningly varied, brutally sensational scenes, . . . alternated with soft interludes in which deathless courage, supreme self-sacrifice, memorable piety, Stoic virtue, and wifely devotion are expected to win favour."[5] Since such a passage might have been written about Rowe's own plays, it is not surprising that Lucan was to his taste. Dr. Welwood's stately Preface to Rowe's translation includes the "Life and Works of Lucan" as well as his tribute to Rowe himself.

Later in the century Dr. Johnson gave his unqualified approval when he wrote, "The version of *Lucan* is one of the greatest productions of English poetry; . . . The *Pharsalia* of Rowe deserves more notice than it obtains, and as it is more read will be more esteemed."[6] Johnson's admiration and comments about the *Pharasalia* remind us that fashions in poetry change from one generation to another. By the time Johnson wrote in 1780, the reading public's taste had turned to the novel rather than to translations of the Classics; and Rowe's translation, while it was still in print, did not fulfill Johnson's prediction. Perhaps the fact that it was written in heroic couplets made it tiresome. Some of Rowe's contemporaries felt that he had expanded the original poem too much, that he had made "two lines" into six verses. Henry Cromwell, writing to Pope, speaks of Rowe's purpose in the poem and his methods: "He [Rowe] is so errant a Whig, that he strains even beyond his Author [Lucan], in passion for Liberty, and aversion to Tyranny; and errs only in amplification."[7] On this point Johnson said of it, "His author's sense is sometimes a little diluted by additional infusions, and sometimes a little weakened by too much expansion."[8]

For a twentieth-century reader, the combination of heroic couplets and artificial language is such that we find it interesting rather than inspiring. Such expressions as "watery eyes" for weeping or "violated oak" for a tree cut down no longer seem elegant to us. Occasionally the violent action is put in memorable verse, as in this description of the man who lost an arm as he clung to the ship:

> Full on his arm a mighty blow descends
> And the torn limb from off the shoulder rends.
> The rigid nerves are cramp'd with stiff'ning cold,
> Convulsive grasp, and still retain their hold.   (III, II. 910–13)

And the imaginative quality of the verse is frequently effective when Rowe describes the strange creatures:

> A basilisk bold Murrus kill'd in vain,
> And nail'd it dying to the sandy plain;
> Along the spear the sliding venom ran,
> And sudden from the weapon, seiz'd the man:
> His hand first touch'd ere it his arm invade,
> Soon he divides it with his shining blade;
> The serpent's force by sad example taught,
> With his lost hand his ransom'd life he bought.   (IX, II. 1405–12)

As always, Rowe's attention to matters of love are handled with skill, as in his description of the enchantress Erichtho and her kind who "Oft, sullen bridegrooms, who unkindly fled/ From blooming beauty, and the genial bed,/ Melt, as the thread runs on, and sighing, feel/ The giddy whirling of the magick wheel" (VI, II. 736–39). And he presents an especially nice passage about Cleopatra and her power over men:

> Mark with what ease her fatal charms can mold
> The heart of Caesar, ruthless, hard, and old:
> Were the soft king his thoughtless head to rest,
> But for a night, on her incestuous breast,
> His crown and friends he'd barter for the bliss
> And give thy head and mine for one lewd kiss;
> On crosses or in flames, we should deplore
> Her beauty's terrible resistless power.   (X, II. 540–48)

It is perhaps Rowe's melodramatic extension of an already melodramatic poem that our modern taste finds unacceptable. But, for our study of Rowe, our view remains that, given his view of his own world and his interest in the extravagant, he and Lucan were compatible. Like *Jane Shore* and *The Fair Penitent*, the *Pharsalia* challenged the Establishment; and, like the violence of rape and murder in *The Ambitious Step-Mother* and in *Tamerlane*, the lurid scenes of battle, of death, of enchantment, and of witchcraft fit precisely Rowe's practice of composition. Again, as we have already observed, Rowe is remarkably consistent in his selection of material and in his handling of it.

II *Rowe's Miscellaneous Verse*

Throughout Rowe's career he wrote occasional verse. Most of these pieces, while they are polished and charming, merely show his skill as a versifier and can scarcely be regarded as serious poetry. Taken together, however, they form an interesting confirmation of our critical view of the plays. Published as *The Poetical Works* (1714), they were included in the various editions of *The Works of Nicholas Rowe* (1727) and in such collections of English poetry as, for example, Alexander Chalmers's *The Works of the English Poets*. On the whole, the poems show the same concern for topical matters, the same clever skill in handling verse technique, and the same support of the Whig principles and the Establishment that we have examined in each of the plays.

Several of the short poems are translations and imitations, and several were published as parts of other work. There are "Songs" and short poems that are in reality *vers de société*. Perhaps Ayre's list of the poetry will serve as an eighteenth-century bibliography. The list reads:

I. *A Poem on the Duke of Marlborough's Victories*. This is an excellent Piece.
II. *An Ode for the New Year* 1717.
III. *Pythagoras's golden Verses*. Done from the Greek. Inserted in the Translation of Dacier's *Life of that Philosopher*.
IV. *Poems on Several Occasions*.
V. His *Translation of Callipoedia*.
VI. *Lucan's Pharsalia. Translated into* English *Verse, with Notes*. . . . This Poet was a great Lover of Liberty, which inclined him to the Translation of Lucan.[9]

An examination of these poems illustrates our thesis that the poems, like the plays, may best be viewed in the context of the precise time in which they were written. The *Poem on the Duke of Marlborough's Victories*, which Ayre lists, was published in folio pamphlet form in 1707: it is the typical panegyric written to celebrate the victories of Marlborough's campaigns by almost every poet and versifier of the day. In this case, the victory is not a specific one but that of a successful year. The fact of the matter is that the poem was first published with the title *On the Late Glorious Successes of Her Majesty's Arms*. Ayre's retitling it *A Poem on the Duke of Marlborough's Victories* is in itself a judgment of the poem as is his comment that he found it an "excellent piece." The second poem on the list—*An Ode for the New Year, 1717*—is a celebration of the "Happy isle: the care of Heav'n/ To the guardian hero given" (II, 310–11), plainly a tribute to George I. The *Callipoedia*, a piece of erotic literature like Ovid's *Art of Love*, one critic has found "is not vulgar but walks a tightrope on the border of prurience most of the time."[10] Ayre's reference to *Poems on Several Occasions* is his listing of Rowe's collected poems.

Rowe says he took some liberty in *The Translation of The Golden Versus of Pythagoras*; they were, he says, "translated at large." A series of axioms, they make a small but complete book of devotions. In the form of couplets the verses begin:

First to the Gods thy humble homage pay:
The greatest this, and first of laws, obey:

> Perform thy vows, observe thy plighted troth,
> And let Religion bind thee to thy oath.   (II, 254)

And Rowe voices in the conclusion Pythagoras's stoic attitude:

> Then if this mortal body thou forsake,
> And thy glad flight to the pure aether take,
> Among the Gods exalted shalt thou shine,
> Immortal, incorruptible, divine:
> The tyrant Death securely shalt thou brave,
> And scorn the dark dominion of the Grave.   (II, 258)

III   *Rowe's Epilogues and Prologues*

Dr. Johnson makes an interesting observation about another group of Rowe's poems when he says "It is remarkable that his prologues and epilogues are all his own, though he sometimes supplied others; he afforded help, but did not solicit it."[11] As for these poems in which Rowe "afforded help," one of the most special instances was the Epilogue spoken by Mrs. Barry on the occasion of a performance of Congreve's *Love for Love* given for the benefit of Betterton, April 7, 1709. Betterton had certainly been a notable actor in Rowe's plays; he had originated the role of Memmon in *The Ambitious Step-Mother;* Tamerlane in *Tamerlane;* Horatio in *The Fair Penitent;* Ulysses in *Ulysses;* and Sir Timothy Tallapoy in *The Biter.* Moreover, Betterton had lent his aid, as we have stated, in collecting the material for the life of Shakespeare that Rowe prefixed to his edition that had been published in this same year, 1709. The benefit was a suitable time to offer tribute to Rowe's good friend.

Rowe also supplied an Epilogue for Farquhar's *Inconstant: or, The Way to Win Him* (an adaptation of Fletcher's *The Wild-Goose Chase*) in which Rowe admonishes the fair to "Turn over ev'ry page of womankind" to gain a husband. Another set piece, a Prologue written for Betterton to speak before Mrs. Centlivre's comedy *The Gamester* (1704), and another one for Mrs. Oldfield to speak before Mrs. Centlivre's *The Cruel Gift* (1707) show Rowe's association not only with the comedy of manners popular in his theater but with the pathetic tragedy of such writers as Mrs. Centlivre and Thomas Southerne.

Rowe's best-known Prologue was written for Colly Cibber's *The Non-Juror* (1717), a version of Molière's *Tartuffe*. The *Non-Juror*, first acted in December, 1717, was quite a sensation; for Cibber had so adapted Molière's play that, as he said,

I borrow'd the *Tartuffe* of *Molière*, and turn'd him, into a modern *Non-Juror:* Upon the Hypocrisy of the *French* Character, I ingrafted a stronger Wickedness, that of an *English* Popish Priest, lurking under the Doctrine of our own Church, to raise his Fortune, upon the Ruin of a worthy Gentleman, whom his dissembled Sanctity had seduc'd into the treasonable Cause of a *Roman Catholick* Out-law.[12]

Cibber's combination of effrontery in using Molière and his vigorous use of the nonjurors, many of whom were Jacobites also, as his principal targets made his play not merely sensational but treasonable by certain standards. Although the nonjurors—those clergymen who at the accession of William and Mary in 1689 had remained loyal to James II and had refused to swear allegiance to the crown—were theoretically nonpolitical, many of them had encouraged the riots in London in 1714–15 and the Jacobite rebellion in Scotland in 1715. In 1717, when Cibber's play was acted, the nonjurors were engaged in defending themselves and their view of ecclesiastical authority in the "Bangorian controversy," a controversy begun by William Law's answer to a sermon preached by Benjamin Hoadley, Bishop of Bangor. Rowe's Prologue aligned him with Cibber, and the sentiments of the play once again supported his views in what he took to be the cause of English liberty. In the verse Rowe says, "Good-breeding ne'er commands us to be civil/ To those who give the nation to the Devil;/ Who at our surest, best foundation strike/ And hate our monarch and our church alike" (II, 276–77). He felt that those who did not wish to be a part of the Establishment should "seek some passive land,/ Where tyrants after your own hearts command" (II, 277).

The poems, then, like the plays, reveal Rowe's interest in the current scene, his association with the small circle of the intellectual elite who made up his intimate friends, and his strong political views. In form and content, they give supporting evidence to the fact that Rowe was typical of the poet–public figure writer who was an important part of the era of Queen Anne. After he became Poet Laureate, the official and occasional poetry that Rowe wrote is of slight importance in a study of his work. For some of it, Rowe had help from friends; and the fact that he was Poet Laureate for so brief a time afforded little opportunity for him to offer any major work.

CHAPTER 10

Conclusion

ALMOST eighteen years after his first play, *The Ambitious Step-Mother*, had been acted at Lincoln's Inn Fields, Rowe lay on his death bed in his house in Covent Garden; instead of a new play at the turn of the year in 1718–1719, his pageant was his elegant funeral as he was laid to rest near Chaucer in Westminster Abbey. In his poem written after Rowe's death, Nicholas Amhurst calls him the "great Recorder of the Brave and Fair," "the Genius of the British Stage," and "the Patriot of a madding Age."[1] These phrases describe quite accurately the reputation Rowe had in his own time.

In the first two decades of the eighteenth century, he was the leading writer of tragedy. Three of the works became stock plays in the repertory theaters, not only in London, but in the provinces as well. *Tamerlane* was performed to celebrate the Whig victories and the Hanoverian succession. *The Fair Penitent* and *Jane Shore* were played throughout the eighteenth century and into the nineteenth. Two of the favorite roles of the celebrated Mrs. Sarah Kemble Siddons were those of Calista and Jane Shore, and the American actress Genevieve Ward played Jane Shore in New York as late as 1890. These three plays illustrate clearly Amhurst's two other phrases also. In *Tamerlane, The Royal Convert,* and *Lady Jane Gray*, Rowe was "the Patriot of a madding age"; and in the characters of Jane Shore, Calista, Lady Jane Gray, Selima, and Ethelinda, Rowe recorded the fair, as he recorded the brave in the characters of Tamerlane, Ulysses, and Guilford.

Rowe was not without critics in his own time. John Dennis called him to account for his lack of conformity to the "Rules." These "Rules" as Dennis saw them ensured a writer's conformity to the traditional approach in observing what was appropriate in the various genres, such as epic, tragic, and lyric poetry, and in following the accepted methods for presenting these genres. As we have seen, Rowe did at first work in the traditional heroic drama of Dryden and his successors and in the drama of sentimental pathos of Otway and Lee; but in each type, Rowe practiced his own variations. He developed in the heroic drama his characters to support William III, the Protestant Succession, and the Church of England as opposed to the Roman Catholic succession of James II and his son James III. In the sentimental pathos of the early plays, Rowe began the later development of the three she-tragedies—*The Fair Penitent, Jane Shore*, and *Lady Jane Gray*.

Charles Gildon, who used Rowe's continuing success to ensure an audience for himself, wrote a play called *A New Rehearsal, or Bays the Younger* (1714), in which all Rowe's plays are wittily called into the "Rules" court. Rowe himself evidently did not heed the criticism since his plays continued to be successful to an audience more concerned with their own tastes and psychological problems than with academic ones. Throughout his work Rowe retained the virtues and the characteristics of the heroic dramas of his predecessors: his plots are dramatically intricate, his heroes speak in proper formal terms, his heroines are beautiful and virtuous—or become so. In three of the plays, *The Fair Penitent, Jane Shore*, and *Lady Jane Gray*, he added the interests of psychological analysis in a series of studies of women in distress.

In *The Fair Penitent*, Calista, through her own unguarded passion, faces a double dilemma. Her lover, having had her on his own terms, will not help her to escape the marriage her father has arranged. For the eighteenth-century audience Calista's dilemma represented an all-too-familiar problem, since for them the attitude of Lothario was the accepted one: a woman who through the weakness of love loses her virtue before marriage is not to be taken seriously and may become, as Calista says, "a wretched wanton . . ./ To toy, and waste an hour of idle time with" (I, 190). Calista does love her father and pity her bridegroom, Altamont. The character of Calista and her relationship to Lothario; the honor of Altamont; the roles of his friend Horatio and Horatio's wife, Lavania, who is Altamont's sister, suggest a complex of family and emotional problems and psychological puzzles that furnished the eighteenth century with a notable masterpiece.

In both *Jane Shore* and *Lady Jane Gray*, Rowe examines in depth the beautiful but helpless woman who is willing to support the principles of loyalty to church and state in such a way that the proper succession of the throne is ensured and the Protestant faith maintained. In both of these plays he also examines the place that the personal responses of love and true virtue have as they become a part of the whole complex of loyalties required to support church and state. Both Jane, the sinner, and Lady Jane, the saint, are subjected to this psychological examination. If *Jane Shore* was the more popular of the two plays, as in fact it was, it must have been because the dilemma of the sinner turned saint was more appealing to Rowe's audience than the saintly Lady Jane, who was bound by the great principles of family loyalty and devotion to her Protestant faith and her country's welfare. Jane Shore's tragedy was the source of endless pity and tears; Lady Jane, less accessible as a woman, became Rowe's final statement of the virtuous fair.

In all his tragedies Rowe added a parable-like didacticism to the melodrama of the Jacobean theater. Calista is to be analyzed; Penelope, to be emulated; Lady Jane, to be admired; Jane Shore, to be forgiven. The "lessons" of the confused Stuart-Hanoverian succession are shown in *The Royal Convert* and in *Ulysses*. The attributes of the ruler are shown and spoken of in the plot and poetry of *Tamerlane, Ulysses, The Royal Convert.* The ideals of loyalty and devotion to the Protestant Church of England are set forth in *The Royal Convert, Tamerlane,* and *Lady Jane Gray.*

Rowe was in every way a man and a writer of his time—to be more precise, of the Whig settlement that brought in William and Mary in 1688 and the House of Hanover in 1714. Rowe and his audience did not require that the theater be separated from the political and moral issues of their day; thus, while Rowe's work is certainly his own in form and technical presentation, all of it clearly reflects the interests and issues of his time. Like his contemporaries Steele, Addison, and Swift, he fashioned his literary material out of his daily concerns. Indeed, as a typical poet-writer-politician, Rowe is perhaps a better mirror of his own time than either Steele or Swift. As one twentieth-century critic has said, ". . . the early eighteenth century may be understood more truly in the work of Rowe than in that of some of his greater contemporaries."[2]

Rowe's blank verse was much admired. In *A New Rehearsal*, while it was said "Nature, Character, and Design, are wholly unknown to him", it was concluded that "a sort of sonorous numerous Verse, . . . has rais'd his Name."[3] Amhurst called him "soft com-

plaining Rowe," and Stephen Hales said that "As a-Poet, he had the
Force of Imagination in a great Degree; just Allusions, proper
Metaphors, and fine Descriptions, are so common with him, and so
much admired, that they are in every Body's Mouth, and need not
my Commendation."[4] And one of Rowe's twentieth-century editors
has asserted that ". . . no living Englishman could write blank verse
more beautifully than Mr. Rowe; no one was better able to give the
proper turn to a just sentiment."[5]

As the eighteenth became the nineteenth and then the twentieth
century, the topical, political material of Rowe's work became less
pertinent to his readers, and Rowe's use of the pathetic characterization and sentimental theories became more noticeable. Even so, a
serious consideration of his work remains necessary for anyone seek-
ing a full understanding of the age of Queen Anne; a knowledge of
his plays is obligatory for anyone interested in the history of the
theater in the eighteenth century; and a familiarity with his work
lends understanding to the reader of Rowe's friends and fellow
writers—of such notable writers as Addison, Steele, Swift, and
Pope. A knowledge of *Tamerlane* (1702) helps to explain Addison's
Cato (1712); they are both polemics in the Whig cause. A consideration of *Lady Jane Gray* (1715) makes a commentary on Steele and his
Crisis (1714) of the preceding spring. For the twentieth-century
student who seeks to recreate the political and religious context of
the first two decades of the eighteenth century, there is no more
valuable source than Rowe's work.

The modern reader finds Rowe's language artificial and his drama
contrived. His *Lucan,* so much admired by Dr. Johnson, has been
forgotten except by the scholars. We are too sophisticated in our
own psychological examination of character to spend much time
with Calista. Yet a review of Rowe and his work will show him to be
surprisingly articulate and skillful in his understanding of both the
body politic and the human heart. In a time when the tyranny of the
powerful dominates government, the sentiments of Artaban as he
becomes the ruler—

> The Gods are great and just. Well have you mark'd
> Celestial powers, your righteous detestation
> Of sacrilege, of base and bloody treachery.
> May this example guide my future sway:
> Let honour, truth and justice crown my reign,
> Ne'er let my Kingly word be given in vain,

> But ever sacred with my foes remain.
> On these foundations shall my empire stand,
> The Gods shall vindicate my just command,
> And guard that power they trusted to my hand.   (I, 78–79)

are still a viable statement for a proper basis of power. Moreover,
Tamerlane's concluding lines as he speaks of Bajazet express the
proper sentiment of the powerful leader:

> Behold the vain effects of earth-born pride,
> That scorn'd Heav'n's laws, and all its pow'r defied:
> That could the hand, which form'd it first, forget,
> And fondly say, I made myself be great:
> But justly those above assert their sway,
> And teach ev'n Kings what homage they should pay,
> Who then rule best, when mindful to obey.   (I, 149)

For the twentieth-century reader, however, Rowe's emphasis on
the role of women and their participation in government, society,
and the family is more important than his political "lessons." From
The Ambitious Step-Mother to *Lady Jane Gray* he created strong,
frequently complex, roles for women, roles offering more than
merely an opportunity for sentimental poetry about tragic or pathetic problems of love. Both Artemisa, the "ambitious step-mother,"
and Rodogune, the Saxon princess, are strong, commanding women
capable of directing men and nations; their selfish ambitions cannot
cancel the vigor of their characters. In Penelope and Lady Jane
Gray, their strength of character lies in their complete loyalty to
their ideals of steadfastness to church and state; the fact that both
Penelope and Lady Jane are too ideal to seem real does not make
them any less useful as models for emulation. For anyone interested
in the developing role of women as they are presented in the drama,
all of Rowe's plays must be carefully examined; the "she-tragedies"
become more than merely the dramatic exploitation of the passions
and positions of women. *The Fair Penitent, Jane Shore,* and *Lady
Jane Gray* are classics in the long and continuing exploration of
woman's place in the public and private segments of our world.

Rowe's vigorous examination of the body politic, his polemics
against tyranny, and his support of his view of the Protestant faith
make a place for him in our ongoing investigation of these timeless
and universal subjects; his discussions of the dilemmas of the

"beautiful fair," his poetic declarations about life, love, and death, and his sympathetic realization of the role of women also insure him the attention of those readers interested in the timeless and universal understanding of the human heart. In both these topics—the body politic and the human heart—we may still claim for Rowe, as his friend Amhurst did, "The best good nature, and the finest Sense."

Notes and References

For the references in the text I have used *The Works of Nicholas Rowe, Esq.*, 2 vols., London: W. Lowndes; J. Nichols; S. Bladon; and W. Nicoll, 1792. There is no modern edition of *The Works*. For the Lucan I have used Nicholas Rowe, *Lucan's Pharsalia Translated into English Verse*, London: Jacob Tonson, 1718.

Chapter One

1. For the biographical material I have used two eighteenth-century *Lives:* James Welwood, "The Preface," *Lucan's Pharsalia, Translated into English Verse by Nicholas Rowe, Esq.* (London, 1718) and Stephen Hales's which was prefixed to *Musarum Lachrymae* (London, 1719). I have supplemented these two accounts with information in Sir Sidney Lee's account in the *Dictionary of National Biography* and in J. R. Sutherland's "Life of Nicholas Rowe" in J. R. Sutherland, ed., *Nicholas Rowe: Three Plays* (London, 1929), pp. 1–37.

2. For information about the Rowe family see Donald B. Clark's unpublished doctoral dissertation, "Nicholas Rowe: A Study in the Development of the Pathetic Tragedy" (George Washington University, 1947), pp. 2–3.

3. Throughout this study I have used as the basis of the historical background for Rowe and his contemporaries George M. Trevelyan, *England Under Queen Anne*, 3 vols. (Fontana Library ed., London, 1965); for the seventeenth century, I have used Maurice Ashley, *England in the Seventeenth Century*, 3rd ed. (Baltimore, 1961); and for the William and Mary period, Stephen B. Baxter, *William III* (London, 1966).

4. See George B. Macaulay, *History of England* (London, 1901), I, 625–30, for a discussion about Monmouth and his followers many of whom were hanged for their rebellion against the crown. Macaulay says that they "were regarded by themselves, and by a large proportion of their neighbors, not as wrongdoers, but as martyrs who sealed with blood the truth of the Protestant religion."

5. See J. R. Jones, *The First Whigs* (London, 1961), for a detailed account of the formation of the Whigs and Tories and for the Exclusion Crisis.

6. See Geroge M. Trevelyan, *The English Revolution 1688–1689* (London, 1938), for a detailed account of the events of the flight of James II and the accession of William and Mary.

7. Among other famous writers who had preceded Rowe at Westminster was John Dryden. For an account of a slightly earlier time at Westminster see Foster Watson, *The English Grammar School to 1660* (Cambridge, 1908).

8. Emmett L. Avery, Arthur H. Scouten, and George Winchester Stone, Jr., eds., *The London Stage 1660–1800* (Carbondale, Ill., 1960–1962) is used throughout for the dates of performances and players of Rowe's plays. See also John Genest, *Some Account of the English Stage from the Restoration in 1660 to 1830* (Bath, 1832).

9. Edward Arber, ed., *Term Catalogues* (London, 1903–06), II, Trinity Term, 1700.

10. See H. W. Pedicord, *The Theatrical Public in the Time of Garrick* (New York, 1954) for an account of this audience.

11. See Avery et al. *The London Stage*, I, p. xliii.

12. Ibid., pp. xix–cxxi.

13. See John Harold Wilson, *A Preface to Restoration Drama* (Boston, 1965), and George Sherburn, *A Literary History of England*, Vol. III: *The Restoration and Eighteenth Century* (1660–1789) (New York, 1948), pp. 748–79.

14. Sherburn, *A Literary History of England*, p. 751. See also Wilson, *A Preface to Restoration Drama*, pp. 67–83, and Eugene M. Waith, *Ideas of Greatness: Heroic Drama in England* (New York, 1971), pp. 269–75.

15. Wilson, p. 58.

16. F. E. Ball, ed., *Correspondence of Swift* (London, 1910–14) II, 41.

17. John Dennis, *Original Letters, Familiar, Moral and Critical* (London, 1721) I, 19–20. Pope also enjoyed Rowe's company; he once wrote, "I am just returned from the country, whither Mr. Rowe did me the favour to accompany me and to pass a week at Binfield. I need not tell you how much a man of his turn could not but entertain me, but I must acquaint you there is a vivacity and gayety of disposition almost peculiar to that gentleman which renders it impossible to part from him without that uneasiness and chagrin which generally succeeds all great pleasures" (*The Correspondence of Alexander Pope*, ed. George Sherburn [Oxford, 1956], I, p. 190). Ayre's account of their friendship is even more explicit; he says: ". . . he was in the Number of *Mr. Pope's* select Friends. Whenever Mr. *Pope* gave any of his Verses into his hands, and receiv'd them from him again, he us'd to say they were like Gold three times tried in the Fire; . . . Mr. *Pope* had a very great Regard both for the Person and Writings of Mr. *Rowe*. . . . The Death of Mr. Rowe affected Mr. *Pope* very strongly, for Mr. Rowe had been of great help to him, was one who took a great deal of Pains to get him Reputation

and by his Praise procur'd him no little Fame" (William Ayre, *Memoirs of the Life and Writings of Alexander Pope, Esq.* [London, 1745] I, pp. 209, 211).

Chapter Two

1. Wilson, pp. 68–71.

2. John Downes, *Roscius Anglicanus or An Historical Review of the Stage* (London, 1708), p. 45.

3. Ibid.

4. The *Bible*, 2 Samuel 11–12; 1 Kings 1: 5–49.

5. See George Wasserman, *John Dryden* (New York, 1964), pp. 103–10, and Charles E. Ward, *The Life of John Dryden* (Chapel Hill, 1961), pp. 149–64 for a discussion of Dryden's use of biblical material.

6. Not until the middle of the eighteenth century, until after the battle of Culloden Moor in 1745 in fact, was the threat to the succession ended.

7. Baxter, *William III*, pp. 381–82.

8. Trevelyan says that Anne had lost at least fifteen children before she came to the throne; and, by that time, 1702, she was already in very ill health. See Trevelyan, *England Under Queen Anne*, I, pp. 178–79.

9. Ibid. p. 134.

10. Ibid., p. 145.

11. During 1701, the quarrel between the Whigs and the Tories increased; the Whigs supported William and the Tories did not; ibid., p. 151 ff.

12. Charles Dibdin, *A Complete History of the English Stage* (London, 1797–1800), IV. p. 295.

Chapter Three

1. Gildon said that the actors were partly responsible for its success; see [Charles Gildon] *A Comparison Between the Two Stages* (London, 1702), p. 190. They certainly contributed, but John Doran, quoted in Sutherland, *Nicholas Rowe: Three Plays*, p. 338, states that "as long as there were Jacobite and Hanoverian parties left this piece survived to receive an uproarious applause."

2. Richard Knolles' *The Generall Historie of the Turkes* (1603) had had an interesting history after its original publication. Editions came out in 1610, 1621, 1631, 1638. Paul Rycaut brought out a revised edition in 1679 and a much enlarged edition published between 1687–1700. This edition was in three folio volumes. Only the first (1603) edition is listed in Rowe's catalogue of books. The original title of the work served as the usual advertisement for such books. It read: Richard Knolles, *The Generall Historie of the Turkes from the first beginning of that nation to the rising of the Othoman Familie . . . Together with the lives and conquests of the Othoman*

Kings and Emperours, etc. (London, 1603). John Savage did an abridgment of the enlarged folio edition; his abridgment was published in two volumes in 1701.

3. Not only did Louis XIV proclaim James III king upon the death of his father James II but in the fall of 1701 the Treaty of the Grand Alliance was signed in September at The Hague. The Allies signing the treaty were England, Holland, and Austria.

4. Downes, p. 45.

5. B. R. S. Fone, ed., *An Apology for the Life of Colley Cibber* (Ann Arbor, 1968), p. 92.

6. As soon as the treaties of Utrecht were signed, the French turned their attention once more to the Jacobite cause, and *Tamerlane* was again pertinent. See Trevelyan, *England Under Queen Anne*, III, p. 268.

7. W. R. Chetwood, *A General History of the Stage* (London, 1749), p. 214.

8. [Gildon] *A Comparison Between the Two Stages*, p. 195.

9. Sutherland, *Nicholas Rowe: Three Plays*, pp. 339–40.

10. Willard Thorp, "A Key to Rowe's *Tamerlane*," *Journal of English and Germanic Philology* XXXIX (1940), 124–27.

11. Waith, *Ideas of Greatness*, p. 272.

Chapter Four

1. Downes, p. 45.

2. Chetwood, pp. 253–54.

3. Sutherland, p. 27.

4. See W. Gifford, ed., *The Plays of Philip Massinger* (London, 1805), III, pp. 453–72 for a comparison of the two plays. Gifford accuses Rowe of deliberate plagiarism, but his argument is too biased to be acceptable.

5. See Donald B. Clark, "An Eighteenth-Century Adaptation of Massinger," *Modern Language Quarterly* XIII (1952), 239–52.

6. [Charles Gildon] *A New Rehearsal: or Bays the Younger* (London, 1715).

7. Sutherland, *Nicholas Rowe: Three Plays*, p. 29.

8. The questions ranged all the way from *"Whether 'tis lawful for a man to beat his wife?"* in the first issue of *The Athenian Mercury* to the one from the young man who wrote: "I'm now courting a young Lady, who is, I think, very agreeable . . . But the mischief on't is, she drinks an unsufferable deal of Coffee, which (according to my Philosophy) I take to be the occasion of her Coyness, and aversion to my Courtship. . . . I'd hope some way may be found out to make her less cruel. Your advice in this matter?" in *Athenian Mercury* XVII (London, 1692), 7.

9. Almost every critic of the play has criticized Rowe for the rather awkward situation he creates between the action and the psychological themes of the play. Dr. Johnson says, "The fifth act is not equal to the

former; the events of the drama are exhausted, and little remains but to talk of what is past." Not until the twentieth century has this act been judged more properly. See Malcolm Goldstein, ed., *The Fair Penitent* (Lincoln, 1969), p. xviii; and Lindley A. Wyman, "The Tradition of the Formal Meditation in Rowe's *The Fair Penitent,*" *Philological Quarterly* XLII (1963), 412–16.

10. Of the three, only Margarete repents; therefore, only she is redeemed.

11. Samuel Johnson, *Lives of the English Poets,* ed. George Birbeck Hill (Oxford, 1905), II, p. 67.

12. The "Prologue" was published anonymously, but it has been suggested that Pope had a hand in writing it.

13. Sophie Chantal Hart, ed., *The Fair Penitent and Jane Shore* (Boston, 1907), p. xiii.

14. "Preface," *The Fair Penitent: . . . As Performed at the Theatre Royal, Covent Garden . . . From the Prompt Book. With Remarks by Mrs. Inchbald* (London, 1807).

15. David E. Baker, *Biographia Dramatica, or A Companion to the Playhouse . . . A New Edition: Carefully corrected, greatly enlarged; and continued from 1764 to 1782 by Isaac Reed* (London, 1782), II, p. 113.

16. Waith points out that in *The Fair Penitent* "Though the characters . . . are inspired by some of the ideals which informed the heroic play in its prime, it requires no subtlety to see that a drastic change has occurred. The old heroes were not 'drooping flowers.' " p. 274.

Chapter Five

1. Johnson, *Lives of the English Poets,* p. 69.

2. Congreve replied to Collier in *Amendments of Mr. Collier's False and Imperfect Citations* (London, 1698).

3. Richard Steele, *Tatler* no. 12, Saturday, May 7, 1709.

4. Ibid.

5. Robert W. Lowe, *Life of Thomas Betterton* (London, 1891), p. 172.

6. Sutherland, p. 31.

Chapter Six

1. Baker, II, p. 393.

2. Joseph Spence's *Anecdotes,* ed. James M. Osborn (Oxford, 1966), p. 96.

3. See British Library Mss. House of Lords: New Series, VI, 246.

4. Johnson, *Lives of the English Poets,* p. 68.

5. Trevelyan, *England Under Queen Anne,* II, p. 96.

6. Ibid., p. 106.

7. Ibid., p. 103.

8. Ibid., p. 106. The Scottish Jacobite, George Lockhart, was probably

correct when he wrote, "They don't so much value in England who shall be King, as whose King he shall be!" Quoted in Trevelyan, op. cit.

9. Ibid., p. 107.

10. Ibid., pp. 96–115.

11. Johnson, *Lives of the English Poets,* p. 69.

12. Ibid.

13. See Trevelyan, *England Under Queen Anne,* II, pp. 164–79, for a discussion of the confusions of the war in Spain.

14. Ibid., p. 81.

15. Ibid., p. 197.

16. Ibid., p. 13.

17. Ibid., p. 245.

18. Ibid., p. 304.

19. Ibid., pp. 337–38.

20. Ibid., p. 338 ff. Anne had, from the beginning, guarded jealously her view of the church as even Swift learned when she refused his ambitions to be preferred to a bishopric. See Calhoun Winton, "Steele, Swift, and the Queen's Physician," in Henry K. Miller, Eric Rothstein, G. S. Rousseau, eds. *The Augustan Milieu,* (Oxford, 1970), pp. 144–49.

Chapter Seven

1. See Sutherland, p. 9.

2. The translation of Nicholas Boileau's *Lutrin* was done by John Ozell, (London, 1708); in 1712 there appeared *Callipaedia, or the Art of Getting Beautiful Children. . . .* Rowe translated the first book, the others being done by Samuel Cobb, J. Diaper, and George Sewell. See Sutherland, p. 9.

3. See, for example, "Colin's Complaint For His Mistress's Unkindness," Sutherland, *Nicholas Rowe: Three Plays,* p. 44.

4. For a recent discussion of Jane Shore in her own time see Samuel M. Pratt, "Jane Shore and the Elizabethans: Some Facts and Speculations," *Texas Studies in Literature and Language,* XI (Winter, 1970), 1293 f.

5. For a detailed comparison of the use of Jane Shore in Shakespeare and in Rowe's play see Hart (Boston, 1907), pp. xxx–xlii.

6. See Trevelyan, *England Under Queen Anne,* III, p. 285, for a discussion of the events of the Christmas time of 1713 with Queen Anne was ill.

7. Such a passage would surely have reminded the audience that, after all, James III was Anne's half brother. In the continuing confusion of the accession, the Tories contacted James III—in fact, just at the time *Jane Shore* was being discussed—to ask that he join the Anglican Church; he refused. Ibid., pp. 286–87.

8. Johnson, *Lives of the English Poets,* p. 68.

9. In the introduction (p. ix) to her edition of *Jane Shore* (1907), Professor Hart says, "Indeed, down to 1880, when Genevieve Ward again played the role, performances of *Jane Shore* are within the memory of many who recall the power which the part had over audiences."

10. [Gildon] *A New Rehearsal*, p. 74. Swift's comment that "I have seen a play professedly writ in the style of Shakespeare wherein the resemblance lay in one single line, 'And so good morrow t'ye, good master lieutenant.'" is a good example of how wrong Rowe's critics should be. The line is from *Lady Jane Gray*, and Swift had obviously missed the pseudo-Shakespearean elements in the play. See Sutherland, pp. 33–34, for a good discussion of the problem.

11. Dr. Johnson was not alone in admiring these lines. Another critic points out that "These few words far exceed the most pompous declamations of Cato." See quotation in Sutherland, p. 352.

12. Alfred Schwarz, "An Example of Eighteenth-Century Pathetic Tragedy: Rowe's *Jane Shore*," *Modern Language Quarterly* IX (1961), 238.

13. Sutherland, p. 36.

Chapter Eight

1. Evidently the press had been pleased with the advertising of *Jane Shore*. See Harry William Pedicord, ed., *The Tragedy of Jane Shore* (Lincoln, 1974), pp. xviii–xix, for a discussion of the pamphlets that were published at the time of the play. Curll, who published *Memoirs of the Lives of King Edward IV and Jane Shore*, printed the passages left out of the play. See Pedicord, p. xiii.

2. Sutherland, p. 36.

3. [Gildon] *The Remarks . . .* "Preface."

4. Dibdin, *A Complete History of the English Stage*, p. 305.

5. Baker, II, p. 183.

6. Ibid., p. 168.

7. For a dramatic account of these last days of Anne's reign see Trevelyan, III, pp. 309–39. See p. 328 for an account of the Dissenters and their joy over the failure of the Schism Act.

8. Sutherland, p. 36.

9. Baker, II, p. 183.

10. This Prologue to *Lady Jane Gray* "Sent by an unknown Hand" is included after the text of the play in *The Works*. See Nicholas Rowe, *The Works*, II, pp. 249–50.

Chapter Nine

1. Welwood, "The Preface," p. xxv.

2. Pope was one of the executors of Rowe's will, in which he left most of his estate to his wife. The will was later published. See *Gentleman's Magazine* I (1822), 208.

3. Norman Ault, *New Light on Pope* (London, 1949), p. 183.

4. Welwood, "The Preface," p. xxi. In response to the dedication the king granted Anne Rowe an annual pension.

5. Lucan, *Pharasalia*, trans., Robert Graves (Baltimore, 1957), p. 13.

6. Johnson, *Lives of the English Poets*, II, p. 69.

7. Pope, *Correspondence*, I, p. 102.

8. Johnson, op. cit., p. 69.

9. Ayre, *Memoirs of . . . Pope*, I, p. 215.

10. Clark, "Nicholas Rowe: A Study in the Development of the Pathetic Tragedy," p. 30.

11. Johnson, op. cit., p. 69.

12. Colley Cibber, *An Apology for the Life of Mr. Colley Cibber . . .* (London, 1740), p. 303.

Chapter Ten

1. *The Poetical Works of Nicholas Rowe, Esq.*, Second Edition, (London, J. Tonson, E. Curll, . . . , 1720), p. 14.

2. Sutherland, p. 21.

3. [Gildon] *A New Rehearsal*, p. 63.

4. Rowe, *The Poetical Works*, pp. 5–6.

5. Sutherland, p. 22.

Selected Bibliography

PRIMARY SOURCES

This chronological listing of Rowe's work in the eighteenth century is followed by selected modern editions.

The Ambitious Step-Mother. London: Peter Buck, 1701.
Tamerlane. London: Jacob Tonson, 1702.
The Fair Penitent. London: Jacob Tonson, 1703.
The Biter. London: Jacob Tonson, 1704.
Ulysses. London: Jacob Tonson, 1705.
The Royal Convert. London: Jacob Tonson, 1707.
The Golden Verses of Pythagoras. London: Jacob Tonson, 1707.
On the Late Glorious Successes of Her Majesty's Arms. London: [N. P.] 1707.
Boileau's Lutrin . . . render'd into English verse. To which is prefixed some account of Boileau's writings and of this translation by N. Rowe. London: R. Burrough, 1708.
Poems on Several Occasions. London: E. Curll, 1713.
The Tragedy of Jane Shore. London: Bernard Lintott, 1714.
The Tragedy of Lady Jane Gray. London: Bernard Lintott, 1715.
Lucan's Pharsalia. Translated into English Verse by Nicholas Rowe, Esq. London: Jacob Tonson, 1718.
The Works of Nicholas Rowe, Esq. 3 Vols. London: J. Tonson 1727.
The Works of Nicholas Rowe, Esq. 2 Vols. London: J. Tonson 1736. Editions in 1747, 1756, 1766, 1792. There has been no edition of *The Works* since the eighteenth century.
The Fair Penitent. Malcolm Goldstein, ed. Lincoln: The University of Nebraska Press, 1969.
Nicholas Rowe: Three Plays. [*Tamerlane, The Fair Penitent, Jane Shore*] James L. Sutherland, ed. London: Scholastis Press, 1929.
Tamerlane, A Tragedy. Landon C. Burns, ed. Philadelphia: University of Pennsylvania Press, 1966.
The Tragedy of Jane Shore. Harry William Pedicord, ed. Lincoln: The University of Nebraska Press, 1974.

SECONDARY SOURCES

ASHLEY, LEONARD R. N. *Colley Cibber*. New York: Twayne, 1965. Excellent study of an important figure in Rowe's theater.

ASTON, ANTHONY. *A Brief Supplement to Colley Cibber, Esq.* London [N. P.] 1748. To be used, as its title suggests, in conjunction with Cibber's own account of himself and the theatrical world of the early eighteenth century.

AULT, NORMAN. *New Light on Pope*. London: Methuen, 1949. Discusses some interesting items relating to Rowe's association with Pope.

AVERY, EMMETT L. *The London Stage, 1700–1729*. Part of the series *The London Stage, 1660–1800: A Calendar of Plays* . . . Carbondale: Southern Illinois University Press, 1960–62. Standard reference for dates of performances in London and for various comments about the plays. Use in conjunction with Nicoll and Genest, below.

AYRE, WILLIAM. *Memoirs of the Life and Writings of Alexander Pope, Esq.*, 2 vols. London: [N.P.] 1745. Has important material about the Rowe-Pope association.

BAKER, DAVID E. *Biographia Dramatica, or A Companion to the Playhouse* . . . 2 Vols. London: T. Walker, 1764. This work has a great many editions, and while it is, as its title suggests, a brief review, it is still a valuable source for the changing view of plays and playwrights. Volume I is a dictionary of playwrights; Volume II, of plays.

BERNBAUM, ERNEST. *The Drama of Sensibility*. Cambridge: Harvard University Press, 1915. Long the standard work on the sentimental drama that developed after Rowe's plays.

BOADEN, JAMES. *Memoirs of Mrs. Siddons*. London: Gibbings and Co., 1893. Some interesting accounts of the celebrated Mrs. Siddons's characterizations of Rowe's heroines.

BOAS, FREDERICK S. *An Introduction to Eighteenth Century Drama 1700–1780*. Oxford: The Clarendon Press, 1953. Chapter on Rowe with facts and background for reading the plays.

BROADUS, E. K. *The Laureatship: A Study of the Office of Poet Laureate in England*. Oxford: The Clarendon Press, 1921. Rowe included in the study.

A *Catalogue of the Library of N. Rowe, Esq. late Poet-Laureat*. London, [1719]. Sale catalogue of Rowe's quite extensive library; list shows Rowe's wide interest in Classical literature, earlier work in English literature, and in French, Spanish, and Italian literature.

[CIBBER, COLLEY]. *An Apology for the Life of Colley Cibber*. B. R. S. Fone, ed. Ann Arbor: The University of Michigan Press, 1968.

CIBBER, THEOPHILAS. *An Account of the Lives of the Poets* . . . 5 Vols. London: R. Griffiths, 1753. An early account of Rowe and his reputation.

———. *Memoirs of the Life of Barton Booth*. London: R. Griffiths, 1753. References to Booth's performances in the Rowe plays.

CLARK, DONALD B. "An Eighteenth Century Adaptation of Massinger." *Modern Language Quarterly*, XIII, 239–52. Discussion of Rowe's use of Massinger's *The Fatal Dowry* for his *Fair Penitent*.

DAMMERS, RICHARD H. "Nicholas Rowe and the Miscellany of 1701." *The Library* LIII (1973), 328–29. Suggests that Rowe and not Gildon was the editor of this miscellany.

DAVIES, THOMAS. *Memoirs of David Garrick*. London, 1780. References to Garrick's performances in Rowe's plays.

DENNIS, JOHN. *Original Letters Familiar, Moral and Critical*. 2 Vols. London, 1721. Dennis was one of the best known of the "Rules" critics, and a friend of Rowe's. The letters are important background material for understanding Rowe.

DORAN, JOHN. *Their Majesties' Servants*. 2 Vols. London: W. H. Allen, 1864. References to many performances of Rowe's plays. Helps understanding of Rowe's importance in late eighteenth and early nineteenth centuries.

DOWNES, JOHN. *Roscius Anglicanus Or An Historical Review of the Stage*. London: H. Playford, 1708. Downes's (the prompter at Drury Lane) account of Rowe's plays is important as a contemporary opinion of the early ones.

GENEST, JOHN. *Some Account of the English Stage from the Restoration in 1660 to 1830*. 10 Vols. Bath: H. E. Carrington, 1832. Information about plays, playwrights, dates of performances, and other such items. Sometimes inaccurate, but a source to be consulted.

[GILDON, CHARLES]. *A Comparison Between the Two Stages*. London: J. Roberts, 1702. Critical discussion of contemporary theater; includes discussion of Rowe's *Ambitious Step-Mother* and *Tamerlane*.

———. *The Life of Mr. T. Betterton*. London: J. Roberts, 1710. Betterton played the roles of Memmon in *The Ambitious Step-Mother*, Tamerlane in *Tamerlane*, Horatio in *The Fair Penitent*, Sir Timothy Tallapoy in *The Biter*, and Ulysses in *Ulysses*. Certainly Betterton is an important figure for Rowe's plays even though this is not an altogether satisfactory account of him.

———. *A New Rehearsal; or Bays the Younger*. London: J. Roberts, 1715. Written in imitation of the dramatic burlesque, *The Rehearsal* (1671), in which Dryden had been satirized by Villiers, Duke of Buckingham. Gildon substitutes Rowe for Dryden, not so successfully done, however.

GOLDSTEIN, MALCOLM. ed. *The Fair Penitent*. Lincoln: The University of Nebraska Press, 1969. Volume in the Regents Restoration Drama Series; includes a good introduction.

HART, SOPHIE CHANTAL, ed. *The Fair Penitent and Jane Shore*. Boston: D. C. Health, 1907. Long introduction comparing *The Fiar Penitent* with Massinger's *The Fatal Dowry* and *Jane Shore* with the historical figure and with Shakespeare.

HESSE, ALFRED W. "Nicholas Rowe's Knowledge of Spanish: A Commentary on Spence and Birbeck Hill." *Papers of the Bibliographical Society of America* 69 (1975), 546–52. Discusses the Spence-Pope story about Lord Oxford's advice to Rowe to learn Spanish.

———. "Some Neglected Life-Records of Nicholas Rowe." *Notes and Queries* CCXX (August, 1975), 348–53 and CCXX (November, 1975), 484–75. Very important information about Rowe and his family.

HUGHES, JOHN. *The Correspondence of John Hughes . . .* 2 Vols. London: T. Robinson, 1773. Hughes was a friend of Rowe's. Letters contain many references to mutual friends.

JACKSON, ALFRED. "Rowe's Historical Tragedies." *Anglia* LIV (1930), 307–30. Survey discussion of Rowe's use of British history.

KEARFUL, FRANK J. "The Nature of Tragedy in Rowe's *The Fair Penitent*." *Papers on Language and Literature* II (1966), 351–60. Excellent discussion of the kind and dimensions of the tragedy in *The Fair Penitent*.

A Lash for the Laureat; or An Address . . . London: [N. P.] 1718. Takes Rowe to task by commenting that "Majesty made cheap, is next uncrown'd."

LOFTIS, JOHN. *Comedy and Society from Congreve to Fielding.* Stanford: Stanford University Press, 1959. One of three books that examine political and social ideas in the early eighteenth century. Valuable for an understanding of Rowe's theater.

———. *Steele at Drury Lane.* Berkeley: University of California Press, 1952. Steele became head of Drury Lane in 1714; study of his time important for an understanding of the last years of Rowe's career.

———. *The Politics of Drama in Augustan England.* Oxford: The Clarendon Press, 1963. Very important book in understanding the importance of politics in Rowe's theater.

Lucan, *Pharsalia.* GRAVES, ROBERT, trans. Baltimore: Penguin Books, 1957. Long, valuable introduction; Graves finds Rowe's rhymed couplets monotonous.

MACMILLAN, DOUGALD, and JONES, H. MUMFORD, eds. *Plays of the Restoration and Eighteenth Century.* New York: Henry Holt, 1931. Representative collection of the most important plays; fine introductions; good notes.

NICOLL, ALLARDYCE. *A History of Early Eighteenth Century Drama, 1700–1750.* London: Cambridge University Press, 1929. Standard, monumental work.

POPE, ALEXANDER. *Correspondence.* George Sherburn, ed. 5 Vols. Oxford: The Clarendon Press, 1956. Pope was a good friend of Rowe's; mentions him or his work frequently in the letters.

Remarks on the Tragedy of the Lady Jane: in a Letter to Mr. Rowe. [N. P., N. D.] Another contemporary comment on Rowe's views; date probably 1715.

ROTHSTEIN, ERIC. *Restoration Tragedy: Form and the Process of Change.* Madison: University of Wisconsin Press, 1967. Important background material for understanding of Rowe's plays.

ROWAN, D. F. "Shore's Wife." *Studies in English Literature* VI (1966), 447–64. Traces the story of Jane Shore in both traditional and formal pieces about her.

SHELDON, ESTHER K. *Thomas Sheridan of Smock-Alley.* Princeton: Princeton University Press, 1967. Important account of Smock-Alley as well as Sheridan. Reveals the extent to which Rowe became a part of the stock repertory.

SUTHERLAND, JAMES L. *Nicholas Rowe: Three Plays.* London: Scholastis Press, 1929. Standard work on Rowe in the twentieth century. Very important. The three plays are *The Fair Penitent, Tamerlane,* and *Jane Shore.*

SWIFT, JONATHAN. *Correspondence.* F. E. Bell, ed. 6 Vols. London: Bell, 1910–14. Swift was fond of Rowe; once recommended him for a government position. Swift's letters important for background and politics.

WILKINSON, TATE. *The Wandering Patentee, or A History of the Yorkshire Theater.* London: R. Robinson, 1795. Incidents and comments about Rowe's plays outside of London.

WYMAN, LINDLY A. "The Tradition of the Formal Meditation in Rowe's *The Fair Penitent." Philological Quarterly* XLII (1963), 412–16. Important for an understanding of the fifth act—the act most critics have felt was unsuccessful.

Index

(The works of Nicholas Rowe are listed under his name)